ICELANDIC KNITS

First published in 2021 by Otava

This English hardback edition published in 2022
by Quadrille. The rights to this book have been
negotiated by Amelie Bennet of Bennet Agency
www.bennetagency.com

Models and instructions Pirjo Iivonen, Tiina Kaarela, Annika Konttaniemi, Niina Laitinen, Merja Ojanperä, Soile Pyhänniska, Anna-Karoliina Tetri and Minttu Wikberg
Technical editing of instructions Heli Rajavaara
Graphic design and layout Satu Kontinen

Published in 2022 by Quadrille Publishing Limited

Quadrille
52–54 Southwark Street
London SE1 1UN
quadrille.com

For the English language hardback edition:
Managing Director Sarah Lavelle
Senior Commissioning Editor Harriet Butt
Assistant Editor Oreolu Grillo
Copy Editor Salima Hirani
Proofreader Marie Clayton
Senior Designer Katherine Keeble
Photographer Miisa Häyrynen, Minttu Wikberg
Head of Production Stephen Lang
Senior Production Controller Lisa Fiske

Cataloguing in Publication Data: a catalogue record for this book is available from the British Library.

Reprinted in 2024
10 9 8 7 6 5 4 3 2

ISBN 978 1 78713 937 4
Printed in China using soy inks

FSC www.fsc.org
MIX
Paper | Supporting responsible forestry
FSC® C018179

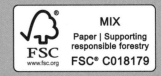

PIRJO IIVONEN
TIINA KAARELA
ANNA-KAROLIINA TETRI
ANNIKA KONTTANIEMI
NIINA LAITINEN
MERJA OJANPERÄ
SOILE PYHÄNNISKA
& MINTTU WIKBERG

quadrille

CONTENTS

INTRODUCTION

In recent years, Icelandic knits have seen unprecedented popularity. The warm and versatile yoke sweaters are quick to knit from thick yarn, and the coloured details are a joy to the eye. The variations are endless.

A genuine Icelandic sweater, known as a *lopapeysa*, is hand-knitted from Icelandic wool and is used as outer wear. Of course, similar knitwear has been used elsewhere in the Nordic countries, and modern Norwegian sweaters have many of the same features that are found in Icelandic knitwear. In this book, eight Finnish designers present their own interpretations of Icelandic knitting. Some of the patterns are more traditional, while others take a much more creative approach to Icelandic knitting.

Icelandic wool repels water, and the thick yarn creates a dense, warm knit. Nothing, however, forces you to use exclusively Icelandic wool. Finnsheep wool is also excellent for these knits, and choosing yarn from a Finnish farm supports small producers in Finland. You can use the recommended yarns for the knits in this book, or substitute them for a yarn of the same weight that better suits your taste or budget. The most important things are that you enjoy the knitting process and that the recipient is pleased with the sweater.

HAVE FUN KNITTING!

ABBREVIATIONS AND TECHNIQUES

RS right side

WS wrong side

MC main colour

CC contrast colour

PM place marker

SM slip marker

RM remove marker

st(s) stitche(s)

k knit

p purl

k2tog knit 2 together – knit 2 stitches together [1 st decreased]

p2tog purl 2 together – purl 2 stitches together [1 st decreased]

k tbl knit through the back (of the) loop – pass the right needle into the back of the loop (instead of the front of the loop) and knit it

M1R make 1 right-leaning (stitch) – using the left needle, pick up the bar between the two stitches at the tips of the needles from back to front, then knit through the front of the loop [1 st increased]

M1L make 1 left-leaning (stitch) – using the left needle, pick up the bar between the two stitches from front to back, then knit through the back of the loop [1 st increased]

ssk slip, slip, knit – slip 2 sts knitwise, one at a time, onto the right needle, transfer them back to the left needle, then knit them together through the back of the loop [1 st decreased]

skpo slip, knit, pass over – slip 1 stitch, knit 1 stitch, pass the slipped stitch over the knitted stitch and off the needle [1 st decreased]

w&t wrap and turn – slip the next stitch onto the right needle, bring the yarn in front, then return the slipped stitch to the left needle, turn work and continue working the short row on the other side. On the next row, when you return to the wrapped stitch, pick up the wrap and knit it together with the stitch it was wrapped around

DS double stitch – hold the yarn in front and slip 1 st knitwise or purlwise (following the pattern) to the right needle. Pull the yarn tightly over the needle and behind the work so that the loop it makes over the needle, sitting next to the stitch you just slipped, look like 2 sts. The next time you come to this DS, comprising a loop and its accompanying slipped stitch, knit (or purl) the loop and the stitch together as a single stitch

cdd centre double decrease – slip 2 sts at once to the right needle as if to knit, p1, pass the slipped stitches over the knitted stitch [2 sts decreased]

STRANDED COLOURWORK

Tension: Many people find that when they switch from using one yarn colour to using two colours or more within rows, their tension (gauge) changes. Before you begin any stranded-knitting project, it is important to knit a swatch in stranded colourwork to check your tension and adjust the needle size, if necessary, to ensure you achieve the same tension in the stranded and unstranded sections of your work and, ultimately, achieve the correct dimensions in the garment you intend to make.

Following charts: When following charted patterns, you may find it helpful to place markers between each pattern repeat, to help you navigate the chart more easily.

Dealing with floats: When switching between colours in a row, and picking up a colour you used previously in that row, draw the yarn across the back of the work to knit or purl the next stitch. The loop of yarn that is created at the back of the work is referred to as a float. If the work requires a float that spans more than 4 stitches, twist the yarns over one another at the back of the work to catch the float and pin it down. This prevents creating long loops of yarn on the wrong side that could catch easily when you put on the sweater.

Yarn dominance: When working in stranded knitting, you will find that, as the different working yarns travel horizontally across the back of the work parallel to one another, the yarn that travels in the lower position creates stitches that are slightly larger than the one travelling uppermost across the back. This fact can be used to great effect – for instance, by using it to deliberately make a specific colour stand out more vibrantly against another. The most important thing with stranded knitting is to always keep your yarns in the same order at the back of the work, so that the dominant yarn does not change in the middle of your colourwork.

WORKING IN THE ROUND

Needles: Many of the patterns in this book are knitted entirely in the round. You will need long and short circular knitting needles of the same size so that, as the number of stitches increases or decreases, you can swap to longer or shorter circular needles. Use the magic loop method. You may also prefer to use double-pointed needles in the sizes stated in the pattern for working sleeves. It is often useful to have more than one set in the same size.

Separating sections: Some of the patterns in this book are knitted from the neck down; others are worked from the hem up. When working from the top down, once you've knitted the yoke, you will separate stitches for the sleeves by transferring them onto waste yarn or a stitch holder, then continue to work the body in the round. You will then return to the stitches reserved on waste yarn for each sleeve, one at a time, to knit those in the round to complete the work. When working from the bottom up, you knit the body and each sleeve separately, leaving the stitches on spare needles or waste yarn as you knit other sections of the garment. Then transfer stitches reserved on waste yarn to a spare needle (of the same size as you are using to knit the project) and knit them off that needle onto your long circular needles to join the body and sleeve sections directly before working the yoke. Ensure you have waste yarn or stitch holders as well as spare needles.

YARN CONVERSION CHART

You may find that you want to use different yarns to those specified in the patterns. See below for the imperial conversions for the metric measurements given.

10 m (11 yd)	125 m (136 yd)	300 m (328 yd)	850 m (930 yd)
15 m (17 yd)	130 m (142 yd)	310 m (339 yd)	875 m (957 yd)
20 m (22 yd)	135 m (147 yd)	320 m (350 yd)	900 m (984 yd)
30 m (32 yd)	140 m (153 yd)	330 m (360 yd)	990 m (1082 yd)
35 m (38 yd)	150 m (164 yd)	360 m (394 yd)	1000 m (1095 yd)
40 m (44 yd)	160 m (175 yd)	380 m (415 yd)	1100 m (1202 yd)
45 m (49 yd)	165 m (180 yd)	400 m (437 yd)	1170 m (1280 yd)
50 m (54 yd)	170 m (186 yd)	450 m (492 yd)	1200 m (1312 yd)
55 m (60 yd)	175 m (191 yd)	500 m (547 yd)	1300 m (1421 yd)
60 m (66 yd)	180 m (197 yd)	540 m (590 yd)	
65 m (71 yd)	190 m (207 yd)	600 m (656 yd)	
70 m (77 yd)	195 m (213 yd)	630 m (689 yd)	50 g (1¾ oz)
75 m (82 yd)	200 m (218 yd)	645 m (705 yd)	100 g (3½ oz)
80 m (87 yd)	205 m (224 yd)	650 m (710 yd)	700g (25 oz)
85 m (93 yd)	210 m (229 yd)	690 m (754 yd)	900g (32 oz)
90 m (98 yd)	220 m (240 yd)	700 m (765 yd)	
95 m (104 yd)	225 m (246 yd)	720 m (787 yd)	
100 m (109 yd)	230 m (252 yd)	730 m (798 yd)	
105 m (114 yd)	250 m (273 yd)	750 m (820 yd)	
110 m (120 yd)	260 m (284 yd)	795 m (869 yd)	
117 m (128 yd)	270 m (295 yd)	800 m (865 yd)	
120 m (131 yd)	290 m (317 yd)	810 m (886 yd)	

"

A small orchid grows in the Lapland wilderness, and that's where the inspiration for this sweater came from. The heath-spotted orchid is found in forested wetlands and peaty meadows – places with scenery that I hold dear. The stranded knitting throughout makes the sweater especially warm. The single contrast stitches also make the plain knit, which can sometimes tend to be slightly tedious, a little more fun. The sweater is knitted from the top down, with short rows in the neck. Why not try out other colour schemes? Even grey could work well here!

Flora

DESIGNER ANNIKA KONTTANIEMI

FLORA

Sizes: S (M, L, XL)

Recommended positive ease 5 cm (2 in).

Dimensions of finished sweater:

Chest circumference: 95 (105, 115, 125) cm
(37⅜ (41⅜, 45¼, 49¼) in).

Length from armpit to hem: 37.5 (38.5, 39.5, 40.5) cm
(14¾ (15⅛, 15½, 16) in).

Length from front collar to hem: 62 (63, 68, 69) cm
(24½ (24¾, 26¾, 27⅛) in).

Circumference of upper sleeve: 32.5 (35, 40, 42.5) cm
(12¾ (13¾, 15¾, 16¾) in).

Wrist circumference: 25 (25, 30, 30) cm (9⅞ (9⅞, 11¾, 11¾) in).

Inner sleeve length: 46 cm (18⅛ in) all sizes.

Yarn (see conversions on page 11): Ístex Léttlopi
(100% wool; 100 m/50 g) or equivalent Aran/
Worsted weight yarn.

MC: 1407 Pine Green Heather 5 (5, 6, 6) balls or
500 (500, 600, 600) m

CC1: 1417 Frostbite 1 (1, 1, 1) ball or 100 (100, 100, 100) m

CC2: 0051 White 1 (1, 1, 1) ball or 100 (100, 100, 100) m

CC3: 1412 Pink Heather 1 (1, 1, 1) ball or 100 (100, 100, 100) m

CC4: 0085 Oatmeal Heather 1 (1, 1, 1) ball or
100 (100, 100, 100) m

CC5: 1705 Royal Fuchsia 1 (1, 1, 1) ball or 100 (100, 100, 100) m

CC6: 9426 Golden Heather 3 (3, 3, 4) balls or
300 (300, 300, 400) m

Needles: Circular needles (80 and 100 cm/32 and
40 in) and double-pointed needles in sizes 3.5 mm
(US 4) and 4.5 mm (US 7).

You will also need: Stitch markers, waste yarn or stitch
holders, and a tapestry needle.

Tension (gauge): 16 sts and 21 rows = 10 cm × 10 cm (4 × 4 in)
in stranded stocking (stockinette) stitch, lightly blocked.

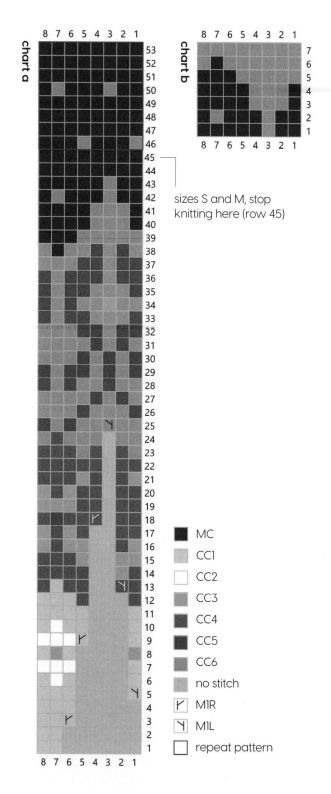

chart a

chart b

sizes S and M, stop
knitting here (row 45)

- ■ MC
- CC1
- □ CC2
- CC3
- CC4
- ■ CC5
- CC6
- no stitch
- ⌐ M1R
- ⌐ M1L
- □ repeat pattern

YOKE

Using 4.5 mm circular needles and CC1, cast on 58 (62, 66, 70) sts. Working flat, *k1, p1, repeat from * to end of row. Join in the round, ensuring not to twist the row of stitches. PM (this is positioned at the centre of the back).

Ribbing: *K1, p1, repeat from * to end of round. Repeat this round until ribbing measures 3 cm (1¼ in).

Work the short rows for the neck:

Row 1 (RS): K18 (20, 22, 25), w&t.

Row 2 (WS): Purl to round marker, SM, p18 (20, 22, 25), w&t.

Row 3: Knit to round marker, SM, k14 (15, 16, 17), w&t.

Row 4: Purl to round marker, SM, p14 (15, 16, 17), w&t.

Row 5: Knit to round marker, SM.

Follow chart A: Using MC and CCs 1, 2, 3, 4, 5, and 6, work the rows of the chart, making increases as indicated. The pattern repeats 29 (31, 33, 35) times per round. Note: **for sizes S and M only:** work chart rows 2–45; **sizes L and XL only:** work chart rows 2–53. When you have completed all chart rows for your size, cut all CCs except CC6. You now have 232 (248, 264, 280) sts.

Next round: Knit the first row of the repeating pattern outlined on chart A (row 46).

BODY

Separate the sleeves: Using MC, k35 (38, 40, 43) sts for the left back section, transfer the next 46 (48, 52, 54) sts onto waste yarn to reserve for the left sleeve. Cast on 6 (8, 12, 14) sts for the left armpit, knit the 70 (76, 80, 86) sts for the front section, transfer the next 46 (48, 52, 54) sts onto waste yarn to reserve for the right sleeve, cast on 6 (8, 12, 14) sts for the right armpit, knit until round marker. You should now have 152 (168, 184, 200) sts.

Follow chart A: Using MC and CC6, work rows 47–53 of the chart, then repeat rows 46–53 until the work measures 29 (30, 31, 32) cm (11½ (11¾, 12¼, 12⅝) in) from the armpit.

Follow chart B: Using MC and CC6, work the rows of the chart. When you have completed all 7 rows, cut the MC.

Ribbing: Switch to 3.5 mm circular needles. Using CC6, *k1, p1, repeat from * to end. Repeat this round until ribbing measures 5 cm (2 in). Cast (bind) off all stitches.

SLEEVES

Transfer the stitches for the left sleeve onto 4.5 mm circular needles. Starting from the centre of the armpit and working in MC, pick up and knit 3 (4, 6, 7) sts, k46 (48, 52, 54) sleeve stitches, pick up and k3 (4, 6, 7) sts, PM. The sleeve should now have 52 (56, 64, 68) sts.

The majority of the sleeve is worked using rows 46–53 of chart A repeatedly. Beginning at row 47, knit 10 (7, 7, 6) rows of the pattern repeat.

Decrease round: Continuing the stranded knitting pattern, work the decrease round as follows k1, ssk, continue in pattern until 3 sts remain, k2tog, k1. *[2 stitches decreased]*

Continuing the stranded knitting pattern, repeat the decrease round every following 11th (8th, 8th, 7th) round another 5 (7, 7, 9) times. You should have 40 (40, 48, 48) sts.

Continue the stranded knitting pattern until the sleeve measures 37.5 cm (14¾ in) from the armpit.

Follow chart B: Using MC and CC6, work the rows of the chart. When you have completed all 7 rows, cut the MC.

Ribbing: Switch to 3.5 mm circular needles. Using CC6 *k1, p1, repeat from * to end. Repeat this round until ribbing measures 5 cm (2 in). Cast (bind) off all stitches.

Set aside and knit the other sleeve in the same way.

FINISHING

Sew in the ends. Wet block or steam block to finish.

"

The Floti (Fleet) sweater is inspired by Viking longships bearing snakes on their prows to ward off any evil spirits encountered on their journeys. As they appear on the horizon, the sun also glints on the row of gilded shields. The sweater is knitted from the top down without seams.

Floti (Fleet)

DESIGNER SOILE PYHÄNNISKA

FLOTI (FLEET)

MODEL SHOWN IS SIZE S

Sizes: S (M, L, XL)
Recommended positive ease 5–10 cm (2–4 in).

Dimensions of finished sweater:
Chest circumference: 90 (100, 110, 120) cm (35½ (39⅜, 43¼, 47¼) in).
Length from armpit to hem: 37 (38, 39, 40) cm (14½ (15, 15⅜, 15¾) in).
Length from front collar to hem: 59.5 (61, 62.5, 64) cm (23⅜ (24, 24⅝, 25¼) in).
Circumference of upper sleeve: 38 (41, 44, 48.5) cm (15 (16⅛, 17⅜, 19⅛) in).
Wrist circumference: 25.5 (25.5, 25.5, 29.5) cm (10 (10, 10, 11⅝) in).
Inner sleeve length: All sizes 46 cm (18⅛ in).

Yarn (see conversions on page 11): Paksupirkka (100% wool; 175 m/100 g) or equivalent DK/Light Worsted weight yarn. Paksupirkka yarn is available in balls of 50 g and skeins of 100 g.
MC: 501 Grafiitti 5 (5, 6, 6) skeins or approx. 800 (875, 900, 990) m
CC1: 210 Naava 1 (1, 1, 1) skein or approx. 110 (130, 150, 170) m
CC2: 222 Curry 1 (1, 1, 1) skein or approx. 100 (110, 120, 130) m

Needles: Circular needles (40 and 100 cm/16 and 40 in) in sizes 4 mm (US 6) and 4.5 mm (US 7), plus circular needles (80 cm/32 in) in size 3.5 mm (US 4), and double-pointed needles in the same sizes.

You will also need: Stitch marker, waste yarn, and a tapestry needle.

Tension (gauge): 20 sts and 22 rows = 10 × 10 cm (4 x 4 in) in stranded knitting on 4.5 mm needles, lightly blocked. Right-side stocking (stockinette) stitch on 4 mm needles 19 sts and 27 rows = 10 × 10 cm (4 x 4 in).

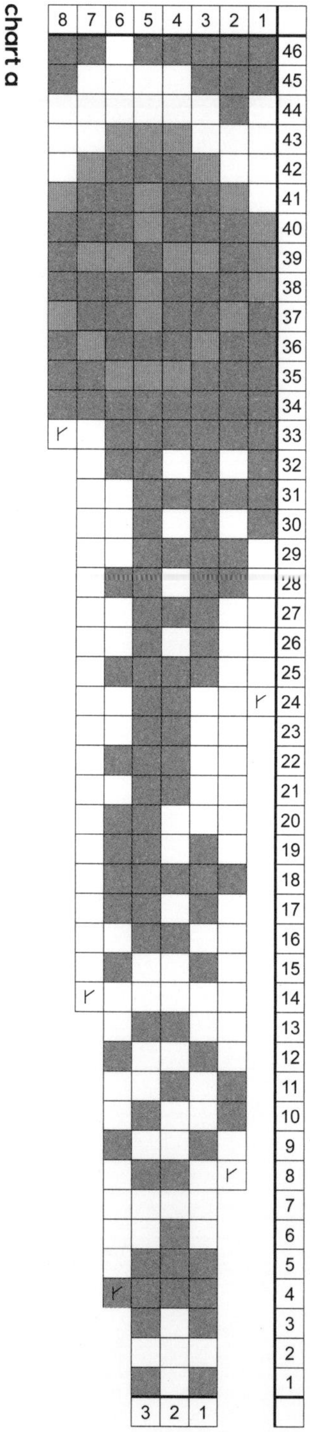
chart a

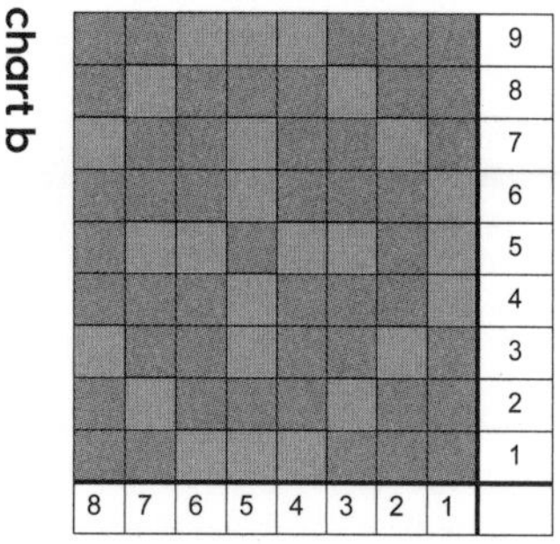
chart b

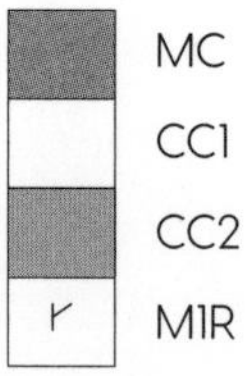
MC
CC1
CC2
M1R

YOKE

Using 4 mm circular needles and CC2, cast on 72 (78, 82, 86) sts. Join in the round, ensuring not to twist the stitches. PM (this is positioned at the centre of the back).

Initial round: Knit to end. Cut the yarn and join MC. Using MC, work 1 round in stocking stitch.

Ribbing: *K1, p1, repeat from * to end. Repeat this round of ribbing 2 more times.

Work 1 round in stocking stitch.

Increase row 1: *K2, M1R, repeat from * to end. You should now have 108 (117, 123, 129) sts.

Work 1 round in stocking stitch.

Size M only:

Increase round 2: *K39, M1R, repeat from *to end. [3 sts increased – 120 sts in total]

Work 1 round in stocking stitch.

Size L only:

Increase round 2: *(K14, M1R) 2 times, k13, M1R, repeat from * to end. [9 sts increased – 132 sts in total]

Work 2 rounds in stocking stitch.

Size XL only:

Increase row 2: *(K11, M1R) 3 times, k10, M1R, repeat from * to end. [12 sts increased – 141 sts in total]

Work 3 rounds in stocking stitch.

Work the short rows for the neck (all sizes):

Row 1 (RS): K27 (30, 33, 35), turn work.

Row 2 (WS): Make a DS, purl to round marker, SM, p27 (30, 33, 35), turn work.

Row 3: Make a DS, knit to round marker, SM, k22 (25, 28, 30), turn work.

Row 4: Make a DS, purl to round marker, SM, p22 (25, 28, 30), turn work.

Row 5: Make a DS, knit to round marker, SM, k17 (20, 23, 25), turn work.

Row 6: Make a DS, purl to round marker, SM, p17 (20, 23, 25), turn work.

Row 7: Make a DS, knit to round marker.

Work 1 round in stocking stitch, knitting each DS on this row as a single stitch.

Follow chart A: Switch to 4.5 mm circular needles. Using MC and CCs 1 and 2, work the rows of chart A, making increases as indicated. The pattern repeats 36 (40, 44, 47) times per round. You should now have 288 (320, 352, 376) sts. After completing all 46 rows of the chart, cut all CCs.

BODY

Separate the body and sleeves: Switch to 4 mm circular needles. Using MC, k40 (45, 50, 53) sts. Transfer the next 64 (70, 76, 82) sts to waste yarn, cast on 6 (6, 5, 8) sts for the armpit. Knit 80 (90, 100, 106) sts. Transfer the next 64 (70, 76, 82) sts to waste yarn, cast on 6 (6, 5, 8) sts for the armpit. K40 (45, 50, 53) sts. The body section now has 172 (192, 210, 228) sts. Continue working in the round in stocking stitch until the body measures 26 (27, 28, 29) cm (10¼ (10⅝, 11, 11½) in) from the armpit OR 11 cm (4¼ in) less than your desired length.

Decrease round: Knit 1 round, decreasing 4 (0, 2, 4) stitches at even intervals. You should now have 168 (192, 208, 224) sts.

Follow chart B: Switch to 4.5 mm needles. Using MC and CC2, work the rows of the chart. When you have completed all 9 rows, cut the CC.

Switch to 3.5 mm needles. Using MC, work 3 rounds in stocking stitch.

Next round: *K1, p1, repeat from * to end.

Repeat this round until ribbing measures 6 cm (2⅜ in). Cut the MC.

Using CC2, work 1 round in stocking stitch.

Cast (bind) off all stitches.

SLEEVES

Use MC and 4 mm circular needles, and starting from the centre of an armpit, pick up and knit 4 (4, 4, 5) sts, k64 (70, 76, 82) sts from the waste yarn, then pick up and knit 4 (4, 4, 5) sts from the other end of the armpit. PM. You should now have 72 (78, 84, 92) sts.

Decrease round 1: K3, k2tog, knit to last 4 sts, ssk, k2.
[2 sts decreased – 70 (76, 82, 90) sts remain]
Knit 6 (5, 4, 4) rounds.

Decrease round 2: K1, k2tog, knit to last 3 sts, ssk, k1.
[2 sts decreased – 68 (74, 80, 88) sts remain]
Repeat decrease round 2 every following 7th (6th, 5th, 5th) round until 48, (48, 48, 56) sts remain.
Continue to work in the round in stocking stitch until sleeve measures 35 cm (13¾ in) from the armpit OR is 11 cm (4¼ in) shorter than your desired length.

Follow chart B: Switch to 4.5 mm circular needles. Using MC and CC2, work the rows of the chart. When you have completed all 9 rows, cut the CC. Switch to 3.5 mm circular needles. Work in stocking stitch for 3 rounds.

Ribbing: Using MC, *k1, p1, repeat from * to end. Repeat this round until ribbing measures 6 cm (2⅜ in). Cut MC.
Using CC2, work in stocking stitch for 1 round.
Cast off all stitches.
Set aside and knit the other sleeve in the same way.

FINISHING

Sew in the ends. Place the sweater in lukewarm water and wet it throughout. Squeeze out the excess water, taking care not to wring the sweater, then place it on a flat surface on a towel, shape it, and leave it to dry.

"

It is simple to adjust the length of the Floti sweater's sleeves and hem to your own measurements.

Ikirouta (Permafrost) is a light, feminine design with delicate lace patterns that give the sweater character. In the patterned areas, you can use brighter colours or as many colours as you like for a different look. Ikirouta is knitted from the hem up. The sleeves are knitted separately and joined to the body at the start of the yoke.

Ikirouta (Permafrost)

DESIGNER PIRJO IIVONEN

IKIROUTA (PERMAFROST)

MODEL SHOWN IS SIZE S

Sizes: S (M, L, XL)

Recommended positive ease 4–5 cm (1½–2 in).

Dimensions of finished sweater:

Chest circumference: 89 (94.5, 100, 105.5) cm (35 (37¼, 39⅜, 41½) in).

Length from armpit to hem: 40 (42, 45, 48) cm (15¾ (16½, 17¾, 18⅞) in.

Length from front collar to hem: 63.5 (69, 73.5, 78.5) cm (25 (27⅛, 29, 30⅞) in).

Circumference of upper sleeve: 34.5 (36.5, 39, 41) cm (13⅝ (14⅜, 15⅜, 16⅛) in).

Wrist circumference: 22 (24.5, 26.5, 26.5) cm (8⅝ (9⅝, 10½, 10½) in).

Inner sleeve length: 45 (48, 51, 53) cm (17¾ (18⅞, 20⅛, 20⅞) in).

Yarn (see conversions on page 11): Sandnes Garn Smart (100 % wool; 100 m/50 g) or equivalent Aran/Worsted weight yarn

MC: 3544 Terrakotta 7 (9, 11, 13) balls or 700 (900, 1100, 1300) m

CC1: 1015 Kitti 2 (2, 3, 3) balls or 200 (200, 300, 300) m

CC2: 2544 Kullanruskea 2 (2, 2, 3) balls or 200 (200, 200, 300) m

Needles: Circular needles (80 and 100 cm/32 and 40 in) and double-pointed needles in sizes 3.5 mm (US 4) and 4 mm (US 6).

You will also need: Stitch markers, waste yarn or stitch holders, and a tapestry needle.

Tension (gauge): 18 sts and 23 rows = 10 × 10 cm (4 x 4 in) in stocking (stockinette) stitch, lightly blocked.

- MC
- CC1
- CC2
- k2tog
- ssk

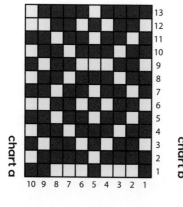

chart a

chart b

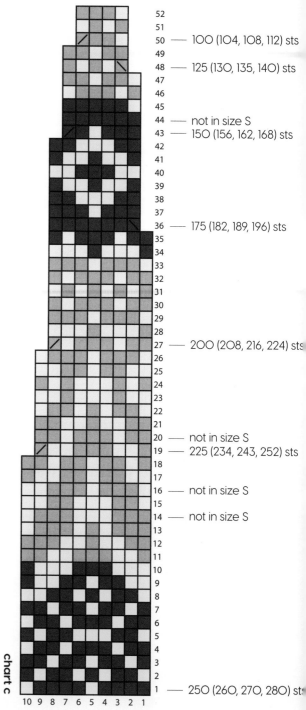

chart c

52
51
50 —— 100 (104, 108, 112) sts
49
48 —— 125 (130, 135, 140) sts
47
46
45
44 —— not in size S
43 —— 150 (156, 162, 168) sts
42
41
40
39
38
37
36 —— 175 (182, 189, 196) sts
35
34
33
32
31
30
29
28
27 —— 200 (208, 216, 224) sts
26
25
24
23
22
21
20 —— not in size S
19 —— 225 (234, 243, 252) sts
18
17
16 —— not in size S
15
14 —— not in size S
13
12
11
10
9
8
7
6
5
4
3
2
1 —— 250 (260, 270, 280) sts

BODY

Using 3.5 mm circular needles and MC, cast on 160 (168, 180, 188) sts. Join in the round, ensuring not to twist the row of stitches. PM (this is positioned at the centre of the back).

Ribbing: *K2, p2, repeat from * to end of round. Repeat this round until ribbing measures 5 cm (2 in). Switch to 4 mm needles.

Work in stocking stitch for 1 round.

Sizes M and XL only:

K42 (47), M1, k85 (95), M1. *[2 sts increased – 160 (170, 180, 190 sts in total]*

Follow chart A (all sizes): Using MC and CC1, work the rows of the chart. The pattern repeats 16 (17, 18, 19) times per round. When you have completed all 13 rows, cut CC1. Switch to 3.5 mm needles.

Using MC, continue working in stocking stitch until the body measures 40 (42, 45, 48) cm (15¾ (16½, 17¾, 18¾) in) from cast-on edge. Set aside the body and knit the sleeves.

SLEEVES

Using 3.5 mm needles and MC, cast on 40 (44, 48, 48) sts. Join in the round, ensuring not to twist the row of sts. PM (this is positioned at the inner sleeve/centre of armpit).

Ribbing: *K2, p2, repeat from *to end. Repeat this round until ribbing measures 5 cm (2 in). Switch to 4 mm needles.

Work in stocking stitch for and knit 1 round.

Follow chart B: Using MC and CC1, work the rows of the chart, When you have completed all 7 rows, cut CC1.

Switch to 3.5 mm needles. Using MC, work in stocking stitch for 2 rounds.

Increase round: K1, M1L, knit until 1 st remains, M1R, k1. *[2 sts increased]*

Work an increase round every 3 (3, 2.5, 2.5) cm (1¼, (1¼, 1, 1) in) a total of 11 (11, 11, 13) times. You should now have 62 (66, 70, 74) sts.

Continue working in the round in stocking stitch until sleeve measures 45 (48, 51, 53) cm (17¾ (18⅞, 20¼, 20⅞) in) from cast-on edge. Transfer 4 (5, 6, 7) stitches from both the start and end of the round onto waste yarn to reserve a total of 8 (10, 12, 14) armpit stitches.

Set aside the first sleeve and knit the second sleeve in the same way.

YOKE

Combine the body and sleeves: Using 3.5 mm circular needles and MC, k36 (37, 39, 40) sts from the body for the back left section. Transfer the next 8 (10, 12, 14) sts to waste yarn for the left armpit. K54 (56, 58, 60) sts to join the first (left) sleeve. K72 (76, 78, 82) sts from the body for the front section. Transfer the next 8 (10, 12, 14) sts to waste yarn for the right armpit. Now join the right sleeve by knitting the 54 (56, 58, 60) sts. Knit the final 36 (37, 39, 40) sts from the body to complete the joining round. You should now have 252 (262, 272, 282) sts.

Decrease round: Knit until there is 1 st left on the left sleeve, k2tog. Knit until there is 1 st left on the right sleeve, k2tog. K to end of round. *[2 sts decreased]* You should now have 250 (260, 270, 280) sts.

Using MC, work in stocking stitch for another 0 (4, 8, 12) rounds.

Follow chart C: Switch to 4 mm needles. Using MC and CCs 1 and 2, work the rows of the chart. The pattern repeats 25 (26, 27, 28) times per round. Note: **for size S only**, omit chart rows 14, 16, 20 and 44. When you have completed all 52 rows of the chart, cut MC and CC1. You should now have 100 (104, 108, 112) sts and the depth of the yoke is 21.5 (25, 26.5, 28.5) cm (8½ (9⅞, 10½, 11¼) in) from the armpit. .

NECK

Switch to 3.5 mm circular needles.

Work the short rows for the neck:

Row 1 (RS): Using CC2, k10 (10, 10, 10) sts, turn work.

Row 2 (WS): Make a DS, purl to row marker, SM, p10 (10, 10, 10), turn work.

Row 3: Make a DS, knit to round marker, SM, knit to DS, knit the DS as a single stitch, k7 (7, 7, 7), turn work.

Row 4: Make a DS, purl to round marker, SM, purl to DS, purl the DS as a single stitch, p7 (7, 7, 7), turn work.

Row 5: Make a DS, knit to round marker, SM, knit to DS, knit the DS as a single stitch, k7 (7, 7, 7), turn work.

Row 6: Make a DS, purl to round marker, SM, purl to DS, purl the DS as a single stitch, p7 (7, 7, 7), turn work.

Row 7: Make a DS, knit to round marker, SM, knit to end of round, knitting each DS on the round as a single stitch.

Decrease round:

Size S only: K3, *k2tog, k2, repeat from * to last 5 sts, k2tog, k3. [24 sts decreased – 76 sts remain]

Size M only: K1, (k2tog, k2) 10 times, (k2tog, k1) 7 times, (k2tog, k2) 10 times, k2tog. [28 sts decreased – 76 sts remain]

Size L only: K1, (k2tog, k2) 12 times, (k2tog, k1) 3 times, (k2tog, k2) 12 times, k2tog. [28 sts decreased – 80 sts remain]

Size XL only: K1, *k2tog, k2, repeat from * to last 3 sts, k2tog, k1. [28 sts decreased – 84 sts remain]

Ribbing: *K2, p2, repeat from * to end.

Repeat this round until ribbing measures 2 cm (¾ in).

Cast (bind) off as follows: K1, *k1, skpo, p1, skpo, p1, skpo, k1, skpo, repeat from * until you have cast off all sts. (Alternatively, cast off loosely.)

FINISHING

Graft the armpits and sew the ends into the wrong side of the work. Wash the sweater in lukewarm water, squeeze inside a terry towel to remove excess water, shape on a flat surface, and leave to dry.

"

The Juurakko (Roots) pattern depicts the winding underground root system of the common madder, a plant that has long been one of the most important sources of natural dyes. Dyers use the roots to make dyes on the red, orange, and yellow colour scale. Madder has been used to dye the yarn used for this project – the dye recipes are provided on pages 42–43.

Juurakko (Roots)

DESIGNER ANNA-KAROLIINA TETRI

JUURAKKO (ROOTS)

Sizes: S (M, L, XL)
Recommended positive ease 6 cm (2⅜ in).

Dimensions of finished sweater:
Chest circumference: 86 (98.5, 111, 123) cm
(33⅞ (38¾, 43¾, 48⅜) in).
Length from armpit to hem (all sizes): 44 cm (17⅜ in).
Length from front collar to hem:
65.5 (66, 67, 68) cm (25¾ (26, 26⅜, 26¾) in).
Circumference of upper sleeve: 37 (40, 43, 46) cm
(14½ (15¾, 17, 18⅛) in).
Wrist circumference: 23 (23, 27.5, 27.5) cm
(9 (9, 10⅞, 10⅞) in).
Inner sleeve length (all sizes): 48 cm (18⅞ in).

Yarn (see conversions on page 11): Vuonue Unelma
(100% Finnish lambswool; 285 tex × 3 = 117 m/100 g)
or equivalent Chunky/Bulky weight yarn.
MC: Luonnonmusta 3 (3, 3, 3) skeins or
260 (290, 320, 380) m
CC1: Krappijuuri 1 recipe I (*see page 42*) 2 (3, 3, 3)
skeins or 220 (260, 290, 310) m
CC2: Krappijuuri 2 recipe II (*see page 42*) 1 (2, 2, 2)
skein(s) or 110 (120, 135, 150) m
CC3: Krappijuuri 3 recipe III (*see page 43*) 2 (2, 2, 3)
skein(s) or 190 (210, 225, 250) m

Needles: Circular needles (40 cm and 80 cm/16 and
40 in) and double-pointed needles in sizes 4.5 mm
(US 7) and 6 mm (US 10).

You will also need: Stitch markers, waste yarn or
stitch holders, and a darning needle with blunt tip.

Tension (gauge): 13 sts and 18 rows = 10 × 10 cm
(4 x 4 in) in stocking (stockinette) stitch on 6 mm
needles, lightly blocked.

BODY

Using 4.5 mm needles and MC, loosely cast on 106 (122, 138, 152) sts. Join in the round, ensuring not to twist the row of stitches. PM.

Initial round: Purl to end.

Repeat this round 2 more times.

Ribbing: *K1, p1, repeat from * to end.

Repeat this round until ribbing measures 4 cm (1½ in). On the last round of ribbing, increase 6 (6, 6, 8) sts at even intervals. You now have 112 (128, 144, 160) sts. Switch to 6 mm circular needles. Work in stocking stitch for 3 rounds.

Follow chart A: Using MC and CC1, work the rows of the chart. When you have completed all 16 rows, cut MC.

Using CC1, work in stocking stitch until the entire stocking-stitch section measures 13 cm (5 in). Cut CC1. Using CC2, work in stocking stitch for 8 cm (3¼ in). Cut CC2.

Using CC3, work in stocking stitch for 13 cm (5 in). Cut CC3.

Using CC2, work in stocking stitch for 4 cm (1½ in). The body length is now 44 cm (17⅜ in). On the last round, leave the last 3 (4, 5, 6) sts unworked and transfer them to waste yarn, RM, transfer the next 3 (4, 5, 6) sts to the same waste yarn for the left armpit.

SLEEVES

Using 4.5 mm double-pointed needles and MC, cast on 30 (30, 36, 36) sts. Join in the round, ensuring not to twist the row of sts. PM.

Initial round: Purl to end.

Repeat this round 2 more times.

Ribbing: *K1, p1, repeat from * to end.

Repeat this round until ribbing measures 4 cm (1½ in). On the last round of ribbing, increase 2 (2, 4, 4) sts at regular intervals. You should now have 32 (32, 40, 40) sts.

Switch to 6 mm needles. Using MC, work in stocking stitch for 1 round.

Increase round: K1, M1R, knit to last stitch, M1L, k1. *[2 stitches increased – 34 (34, 42, 42) in total]* (You will repeat this increase round while working the chart and on up the sleeve every following 9th (8th, 9th, 8th) round a further 7 (9, 7, 9) times until you have 48 (52, 56, 60) sts.

Work in stocking stitch for 1 round.

Follow chart A: Using MC and CC1, work the rows of the chart. *At the same time, continue making increases as described above.* Note that the pattern will not distribute evenly due to the increases. To account for this, always ensure you begin working on the chart at the same position on the round. Place a stitch marker at the start of the first pattern repeat to guide you. When you have completed all 16 rows of the chart A, cut MC.

Using CC1, work in stocking stitch for 13 cm (5⅛ in). Cut CC1.

Using CC2, work in stocking stitch for 4 cm (1½ in). Using CC3, work in stocking stitch for 21 cm (8¼ in). Cut CC3. Using CC2, work in stocking stitch for 4 cm (1½ in). The length of the sleeve is now 48 cm (18⅞ in). Cut CC2. Transfer the 3 (4, 5, 6) sts before the round marker to waste yarn, RM, transfer the next 3 (4, 5, 6) sts to the same waste yarn to reserve a total of 6 (8, 10, 12) sts for the armpit.

Set aside and knit the other sleeve in the same way.

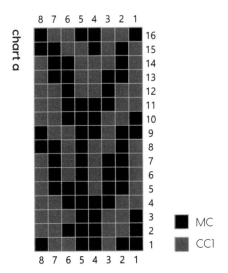

chart a

MC

CC1

YOKE

Combine the body and sleeves: Using 6 mm
needles and CC1, knit the 42 (44, 46, 48) sts of one
sleeve (this will be the left sleeve). K50 (56, 62, 68) sts
for the front section. Transfer the next 6 (8, 10, 12) sts
to waste yarn to reserve for the right armpit, knit
the 42 (44, 46, 48) sts of the second (right) sleeve,
k50 (56, 62, 68) sts for the back section, PM (this
is positioned at the left armpit). You should now
have 184 (200, 216, 232) sts.
Work in stocking stitch for 2 rounds.
Follow chart B: Using MC and CC1, follow the
chart, decreasing stitches as indicated. The pattern
repeats 23 (25, 27, 29) times per round. Note: **for size
S only,** skip rows 32 and 36; **for size M only,** skip row
32. Once you have completed rows all 39 rows
of chart B, you should have 69 (75, 81, 87) sts.
Size XL only: Using MC, work in stocking stitch
for 2 rounds.
Decrease round (all sizes): Switch to 4.5 mm
circular needles. Using MC, decrease 3 (5, 7, 7) sts at
regular intervals. You should have 66 (70, 74, 80) sts.
Ribbing: *K1, p1, repeat from * to end.
Repeat this row until ribbing measures 2 cm (¾ in).
Next round: Using CC1 yarn, work in garter stitch
for 2 cm (¾ in).
Cast (bind) off loosely.

FINISHING

Graft the armpit sts. Sew in the ends. Dampen
the sweater, shape it, and then leave to dry.

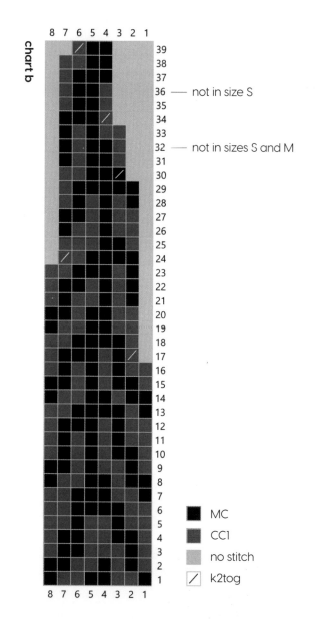

chart b

— not in size S

— not in sizes S and M

■ MC
■ CC1
  no stitch
╱ k2tog

"

It's easy to tell that the yarns for
Juurakko were dyed with madder root
(*Rubia tinctorum*). The colour produced
by the plant is vibrant, so you can dye an
entire sweater with just 300 g (10½ oz)
of the chopped root. Aside from being
pleasing to the eye and complementing
one another, the colours do not easily
fade or run, so dyeing the yarn for the
sweater yourself means the colours
will stay vibrant from year to year.

PRE-MORDANTING AND DYEING YARN

The yarn used to make the Juurakko sweater was dyed using natural dyestuffs. The first stage of the process is to treat the yarn you wish to dye with a dye fixative, a process known as pre-mordanting. Without this fixative, the dye will not bind to the yarn permanently. The following instructions for mordanting (*see below*) and dyeing (*see pages 42–43*) are meant for batches of 100 g (3½ oz) yarn (which should be weighed when it is dry). Adjust the quantities of water, mordant, and dyestuff to suit the weight of the yarn you wish to dye to use for your own Juurakko sweater. Pre-mordanting and dyeing in the main colour should be carried out in several batches (unless you have an extremely large dye bath available). Dyeing with too little liquid will create an uneven result. Use a dedicated steel cooking pan with a large enough capacity (in the region of 8–10 litres (8½–10½ US quarts)).

PRE-MORDANTING

1. Before dyeing, weigh the yarn to establish the dry weight, then carefully wash it at a cool temperature using a wool detergent or a neutral detergent. This will remove dirt (such as spinning oil) that would otherwise prevent the dye from binding to the yarn.

2. Measure out 10% alum and 5% cream of tartar in relation to the dry weight of the yarn e.g. 10 g (⅓ oz) alum and 5 g (⅙ oz) cream of tartar per 100 g (3½ oz) yarn.

3. Measure 5 litres (5¼ US quarts) water per 100 g (3½ oz) yarn and pour it into a dye bath. There should be enough water to completely cover the yarn and you should be able to move the yarn around easily in the dye bath.

4. Dissolve the weighed mordants together in a small quantity of boiling water. Set aside.

5. Using thread, bind the skein of yarn at about four points equally spaced around the circumference, then attach a rug rag or similar to one of the binds. You will use this as a cord to move the skein of yarn around in the dye bath.

6. Heat the water in the dye bath to 30°C (86°F). Place the yarn in the dye bath and hang the cord from a stick that spans the diameter of the dye bath and overlaps the edges. Now heat the water to 40°C (104°F). Lift the skein out of the water temporarily and add the dissolved mordants into the hot water. Mix well.

7. Place the yarn back into the dye bath. Heat the water slowly until it reaches 80–90°C (176–194°F). (Avoid rapid changes in temperature to prevent the yarn from felting. Also, do not let the water boil, as this may cause the yarn to felt and become damaged.) Maintain this temperature for 1 hour. Move the yarn from time to time to allow the mordants to bind to the yarn evenly.

8. Switch off the heat and allow the yarn to cool in the mordanting water overnight if possible. Again, avoid rapid temperature changes – if you try to cool the yarn with cold water, it will felt. If overnight cooling is not possible, you can take the yarn out of the mordanting water and let cool at room temperature.

9. Rinse the cooled yarn thoroughly (*see page 43*) before you begin to dye it. Alternatively, let it dry, then store the yarn until you are ready to dye. Pre-mordant all of the yarn you need for your sweater in the same way before you begin dyeing.

RECIPE I
CC1, DYER'S MADDER ROOT, FIRST BATH (RED)

Ratio 1:1, i.e., 100 g (3½ oz) dried dyer's madder root Rubia tinctorum), chopped, per 100 g (3½ oz) yarn (dry weight).

---

1. Put the chopped madder root into your dye bath and add 3 litres (3¼ US quarts) water per 100 g (3½ oz) yarn (dry weight). Leave to soak for 12–24 hours.

2. Place the dye bath on the heat source. Moisten the pre-mordanted yarn and add it to the dye bath containing the swollen pieces of dyer's madder root.

3. Turn on the heat and slowly increase the temperature until it reaches 50–60°C (122–140°F). Maintain this temperature for 3 hours.

4. Remove the dye bath from the heat source. Leave the yarn in the dye bath overnight to cool.

5. Carefully lift the yarn out of the dye bath. Shake all of the madder root pieces off the yarn and return them to the dye bath. Reserve this dye bath for the first afterbath (see *recipe II, right*).

6. Rinse the dyed yarn in lukewarm water (see *opposite page*). Dry the yarn flat on a drying rack.

RECIPE II
CC2, DYER'S MADDER ROOT FIRST AFTERBATH (STRONG ORANGE)

Use the reserved dye bath from recipe I to make a strong orange. Use the same quantity of yarn you dyed in the first batch.

---

1. Check the volume of liquid left in the dye bath. If necessary, top it up with water to 3 litres (3¼ US quarts) liquid per 100 g (3½ oz) yarn.

2. Place the dye bath on the heat source. Moisten the pre-mordanted yarn and add it to the dye bath containing the common madder root.

3. Turn on the heat and slowly increase the temperature until it reaches 45–55°C (113–131°F). Maintain this temperature for 3 hours.

4. Remove the dye bath from the heat source. Leave the yarn in the dye bath overnight to cool.

5. Carefully lift the yarn out of the dye bath. Shake all of the madder root pieces off the yarn and return them to the dye bath. Reserve the dye bath for the first afterbath (see *recipe III, opposite page*).

6. Rinse the dyed yarn in lukewarm water (see *opposite page*). Dry the yarn flat on a drying rack.

RECIPE III
CC3, DYER'S MADDER ROOT SECOND AFTERBATH (PALE ORANGE)

Use the reserved dye bath from recipe II to make a pale orange. Use the same quantity of yarn you dyed in the previous batches.

1. Check the volume of liquid left in the dye bath. If necessary, top it up with water to 3 litres (3¼ US quarts) liquid per 100 g (3½ oz) yarn.

2. Place the dye bath on the heat source. Moisten the pre-mordanted yarn and add it to the dye bath containing the common madder root.

3. Turn on the heat and slowly increase the temperature until it reaches 45–55°C (113–131°F). Maintain this temperature for 3 hours.

4. Remove the dye bath from the heat source. Leave the yarn in the dye bath overnight to cool

5. Carefully lift the yarn out of the dye bath. Shake all of the madder root pieces off the yarn. Rinse the dyed yarn in lukewarm water (see right). Dry the yarn flat on a drying rack.

PLEASE NOTE!

Achieving colour gradient: When you reserve a used dye bath in order to reuse the dyestuffs for subsequent afterbaths, the results from each afterbath will be progressively paler.

To make the Juurakko sweater, you need a smaller amount of CC2 than CC1. Once you have dyed CC1, it is safe to use the reserved afterbath for a smaller quantity of yarn to create CC2 – you will still achieve the desired paler shade.

Uneven dyeing: The roots and yarn may mix in the dye bath. Don't be concerned by this. The aim is to achieve an uneven dyeing result. The yarn that comes into contact with the dyestuff will be dyed more vibrantly. This will help you achieve beautiful flecks of colour throughout the orange areas of the sweater, yet still achieve the desired colour gradient across the entire sweater.

Temperature: When dyeing with dyer's madder root, a low temperature, as used here, produces clean reds and oranges. If the dyeing temperature is high, the colour turns a reddish-brown. Ensure you follow the temperature guidelines provide here to achieve the correct colours.

Rinsing: When rinsing mordanted or dyed yarn, the temperature of the water is important, because rapid cooling in cold water may cause felting. Never put warm yarn into cold water. Use a bucket filled with lukewarm water, and change the water as many times as needed until the rinsing water is clear. Add a capful of vinegar to the last rinse – the added acidity is good for the yarn. After the rinse, the yarn can be washed lightly with wool soap and rinsed again in the same way.

Keltainen kukkula is a variation of a traditional Icelandic knitting pattern to which I've added my own favourite elements. The Fair Isle pattern is traditionally Finnish, from the 19th century, and is used all over the country, especially in socks and mittens. Depending on the region, this tactile surface is referred to as either puffattu (puffed) or rokokas (pockmarked). As a hood enthusiast, I also decided to add a hood to keep the wearer warm.

Keltainen kukkula (Yellow Hillock)

DESIGNER ANNA-KAROLIINA TETRI

KELTAINEN KUKKULA (YELLOW HILLOCK)

MODEL SHOWN IS SIZE L

Sizes: S (M, L, XL)

Recommended positive ease approx. 6 cm (2⅜ in).

Dimensions of finished sweater:

Chest circumference: 92.5 (101.5, 111, 120) cm (36⅜ (40, 43¾, 47¼) in).

Length from armpit to hem: 43 cm (17 in).

Length from front collar to hem: 64.5 (65.5, 66.5, 67.5) cm (25⅜ (25¾, 26¼, 26⅝) in).

Circumference of upper sleeve: 37 (38.5, 43, 44.5) cm (14½ (15⅛, 17, 17½) in).

Wrist circumference: 24.5 (24.5, 29, 29) cm (9⅝ (9⅝, 11½, 11½) in).

Inner sleeve length: 48 cm (18⅞ in).

Yarn (see conversions on page 11): Vuonue Unelma (100% Finnish lambswool; 285 tex × 3 = 117 m/100 g) or equivalent Chunky/Bulky weight yarn.

MC: Yellow reseda (recipe I) (*see page 50*) 6 (6, 7, 7) skeins or 645 (690, 750, 795) m

CC1: Grey Aleppo oak (recipe II) (*see page 50*) 2 (2, 2, 2) skeins or 170 (180, 195, 205) m

CC2: Carmine cochineal (recipe III) (*see page 51*) 1 (1, 1, 1) skein or 45 (50, 50, 55) m

CC3: Purple cochineal (recipe IV) (*see page 51*) 1 (1, 1, 1) skein or 40 (45, 45, 50) m

CC4: Reddish yellow cochineal (recipe V) (*see page 51*) 1 (1, 1, 1) skein or 35 (35, 40, 40) m

Needles: Circular needles (40 and 80 cm/16 and 32 in) and double-pointed needles in sizes 4.5 mm (US 7) and 6 mm (US 10).

You will also need: Stitch markers, waste yarn or stitch holders, and a darning needle with blunt tip.

Tension: 13 sts and 18 rows = 10 × 10 cm (4 x 4 in) in stocking (stockinette) stitch on 6 mm needles, and 13 sts and 24 rows = 10 × 10 cm in stranded knitting on 6 mm needles, lightly blocked.

chart a

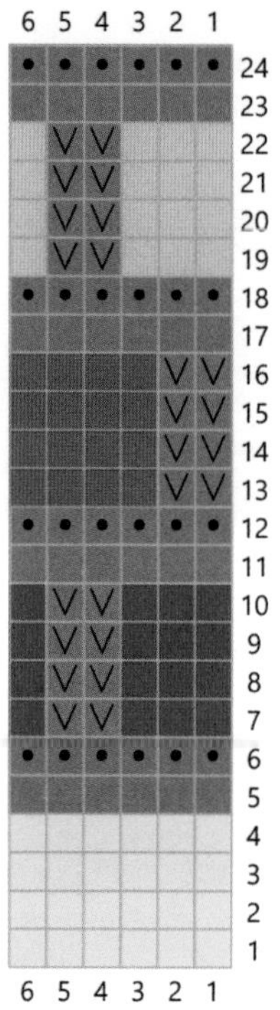

chart b

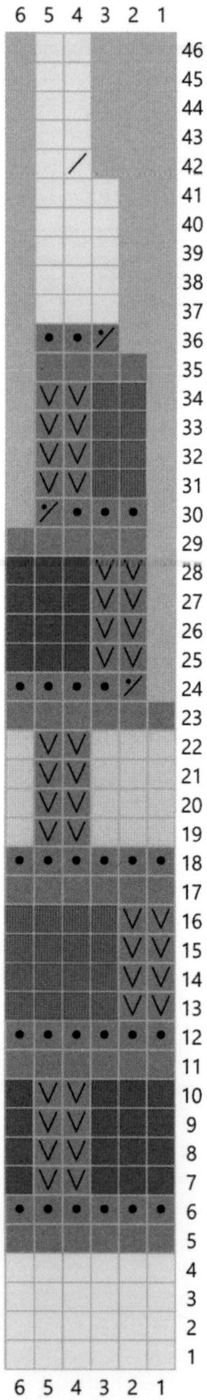

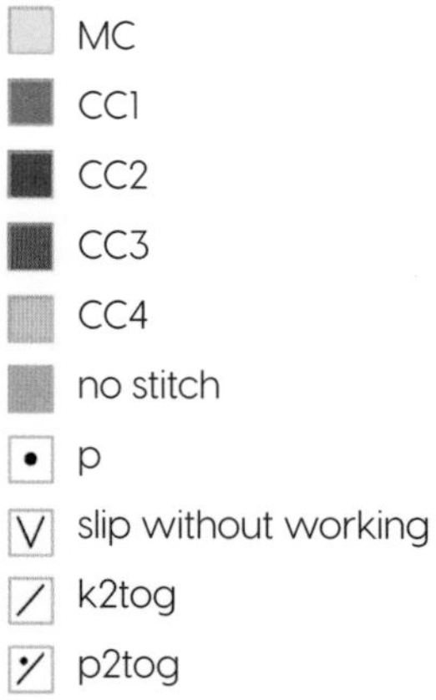

MC
CC1
CC2
CC3
CC4
no stitch
p
slip without working
k2tog
p2tog

BODY

Using 4.5 mm needles and MC, loosely cast on 114 (126, 138, 148) sts. Join in the round, ensuring not to twist the row of stitches. PM (this is positioned at the left side).

Ribbing: *K1, p1, repeat from * to end.
Repeat this round until ribbing measures 5 cm (2 in). On the last round of ribbing, increase 6 (6, 6, 8) sts at even intervals. You should now have 120 (132, 144, 156) sts.

Follow chart A: Switch to 6 mm circular needles. Using MC and CCs 1, 2 and 3, work the rows of the chart. When you have completed all 24 rows, cut all CCs.

Using MC, continue in stocking stitch until the body measures 43 cm (17 in). On the last round, leave the last 2 (3, 4, 5) sts unworked and transfer them to waste yarn, RM. Transfer the next 2 (3, 4, 5) sts to the same waste yarn for the armpit.

Set the work aside and knit the sleeves.

SLEEVES

Using 4.5 mm needles and MC, cast on 32 (32, 38, 38) sts. Join in the round, ensuring not to twist the row of stitches. PM (this is positioned at the inner sleeve).

Ribbing: *K1, p1, repeat from * to end.
Repeat this round until ribbing measures 5 cm (2 in). On the last round of ribbing, increase 4 sts at even intervals. You should now have 36 (36, 42, 42) sts.

Follow chart A/work the sleeve increases: Switch to 6 mm needles. Using MC and CCs 1, 2, 3, and 4, work the rows of chart A. The pattern repeats 6 (6, 7, 7) times per round. At the same time, work the sleeve increases. Increase rows are as follows: K1, M1R, k to 1 st before end of round, M1L, k1. Work the first increase round on the second row of the chart, then on every following 10th (8th, 8th, 8th) round a further 5 (6, 6, 7) times. You should now have 48 (50, 56, 58) sts. Note that the sleeve pattern

will not distribute evenly due to the increases. At the beginning of an increase round, always ensure you account for the increase and begin working on the charted pattern at the same point on the sleeve circumference. Place a stitch marker at the start of the first pattern repeat when you work chart row 1 (this will be with the round marker until the first increase row) so you always begin working the chart at the correct place on your sleeve. Once you have completed all 24 rows of the chart, cut the CCs. Using MC, continue working in stocking stitch, making increases as outlined above, until the sleeve measures 48 cm (18⅞ in). Cut the MC.

Transfer the 3 (3, 5, 5) sts before the round marker to waste yarn, RM, then transfer the next 2 (2, 4, 4) sts to the same waste yarn to reserve a total of 5 (5, 9, 9) sts for the armpit.

Set aside and knit the other sleeve in the same way.

YOKE

Join the body and sleeves: Using 6 mm circular needles, knit the first sleeve's 43 (45, 47, 49) sts (this will be the right sleeve), PM (right back marker, positioned at the point at which the right sleeve meets the right back). Knit 56 (60, 64, 68) sts for the back section. Transfer the next 4 (6, 8, 10) sts to waste yarn for the left armpit, PM (left back, where left back meets left sleeve), knit the second sleeve's 43 (45, 47, 49) sts, PM (left front), knit the front section's 56 (60, 64, 68) stitches, PM (this is the new round marker). You should now have 198 (210, 222, 234) sts.

Follow chart B: Using MC and CCs 1, 2, and 3, work the rows of the chart, making decreases as indicated. Once you have completed all 46 of the chart, cut the CCs, you should have 66 (70, 74, 78) sts. Using MC, work in stocking stitch for 3 (5, 7, 9) rounds.

NECK AND HOOD

Decrease round: Continuing in stocking stitch, decrease 10 sts evenly (2 sts from each sleeve and 3 sts from both the front and back sections). You will be left with 56 (60, 64, 68) sts.

Mark the centre of the front section with a stitch marker and knit to it.

Ribbing: Switch to 4.5 mm circular needles.*K1, p1, repeat from * to end of round.

Repeat this round until ribbing measures 3 cm (1¼ in).

Next round: Switch to 6 mm circular needles. Knit to end. Pick up and knit 3 sts from the front section you just knitted so that the new stitches overlap with them. The hood now has a total of 59 (63, 67, 71) sts. Mark the centre st on the hood (the 30th (32nd, 34th, 36th) st) with a stitch marker.

Work the hood increases: The hood is worked flat in stocking stitch, with the edge stitch always knitted on both the RS and WS.

The hood increases and decreases are worked on both sides of the centre stitch on the RS.

Increase row (RS): *Knit to centre stitch, M1R, knit centre stitch, M1L, knit to end.

Next row (WS): K1, p to 1 st before end, k1. Repeat the last 2 rows 5 more times. You should now have 71 (75, 79, 83) sts.

Continue in stocking stitch, knitting all 4 edge sts on each row, until the hood measures 22 cm (8⅝ in).

Work the hood decreases: Decreases are knitted on both sides of the centre stitch on the RS.

Decrease row (RS): Knit to 4 sts before the centre stitch, k2tog, k5, ssk, knit to end of row.

Next row (WS): Purl to end.

Repeat the last 2 rows 15 more times. You should now have 39 (43, 47, 51) sts.

Divide the hood sts equally into 2 sections and transfer one section onto a separate needle. Turn the hood inside so the right sides of the two halves of the hood are facing one another. The last stitch you knitted should be on the back needle. Cast (bind) off the stitches using the 3-needle cast off, or graft them together. As the number of stitches is odd, the last two front-most stitches are bound off at the same time.

Using 4.5 mm circular needle and MC, pick up 68 sts from the edge of the hood.

Ribbing: *K1, p1, repeat from * to end. Repeat the last row until ribbing measures approximately 2 cm (¾ in). Cast off loosely.

FINISHING

Graft the armpits. Sew in the ends. Dampen the sweater, shape it, and then leave to dry.

> Keltainen kukkula's colours come from nature. Reseda, Aleppo oak, and cochineal have been used as dyestuffs for millennia, and all have good colour and light fastness.

RECIPE I
MC, RESEDA (YELLOW)

Ratio 1:2, i.e., 50 g (1¾ oz) chopped dried weld plant to 100 g (3½ oz) yarn (dry weight). Use 1 tbsp sodium carbonate (soda ash) as an assist

1. You need a dedicated steel cooking pan to use as a dye bath. Put the weld into the dye bath and add approximately 3 litres (3¼ US quarts) water. Leave to soak overnight.

2. Put the dye bath on your heat source and bring the liquid to a boil, then simmer for 30 minutes. After this, stir in 1 tbsp soda ash.

3. Cook out the dye for 2 hours.

4. Strain out and discard the dyestuff, then measure the remaining liquid and return it to the pan. Using water, top up the liquid to 5 litres (5¼ US quarts) per 100 g (3½ oz) yarn (dry weight). Leave to cool to 30°C (86°F) – the dye liquid is likely to be hotter than this, despite being topped up with cold water.

5. When the dye liquid is at 30°C (86°F), place the pre-mordanted and dampened yarn into it. Slowly increase the temperature to 70–80°C (158–176°F). Maintaining this temperature, dye for 2 hours.

6. Take the dye bath off the heat source. Leave the yarn in the dyeing liquid to cool overnight.

7. Remove the yarn from the dyeing liquid, reserving the liquid to use as an afterbath for Recipe V (see opposite). Rinse the yarn (see page 43) and dry flat.

Note: You need 600–700 g (21¼–24¾oz) of MC to make the Keltainen kukkula sweater, so unless you have a huge dye bath, you will need to dye the yellow yarn in several batches.

RECIPE II
CC1, OAK (GREY)

Ratio 1:5, i.e., 20 g (⅔ oz) powdered oak galls to 100 g (3½ oz) yarn (dry weight). Use 5% of the dry weight of the yarn (5 g/⅙ oz) iron mordant (ferrous sulphate) as a post-mordant

1. Put the powdered oak galls into a dye bath and add approximately 3 litres (3¼ US quarts) water. Bring to a boil, then simmer for 1 hour.

2. Strain the liquid through muslin (cheesecloth), then measure it and return it to the pan. Using water, top up the liquid to 5 litres (5¼ quarts) per 100 g (3½ oz) yarn (dry weight). Leave to cool to 30°C (86°F) – the dye liquid is likely to be hotter than this, despite being topped up with cold water.

3. When the dye liquid is at 30°C (86°F), place the pre-mordanted and dampened yarn into it. (Note that, at this point, both the liquid and the yarn will look very dull – don't be concerned by this.) Slowly increase the temperature to 70–80°C (158–176°F). Maintaining this temperature, dye for 1 hour.

4. Carefully lift the yarn out of the dye temporarily. Add the iron mordant to the hot liquid and mix thoroughly. Return the yarn to the dye bath. Maintaining the same temperature (70–80°C (158–176°F), dye for 15 minutes.

5. Remove the yarn from the dye bath. Leave it in a bucket to cool, then rinse (see page 43) and dry flat.

RECIPE III
CC2, COCHINEAL (CARMINE RED)

7 g (¼ oz) cochineal powder per 100 g (3½ oz) yarn

1. Put the cochineal powder into a dye bath and add approximately 3 litres (3¼ US quarts) water. Bring to a boil, then simmer for 1 hour.

2. Strain the liquid through muslin (cheesecloth), then measure it and return it to the pan. Using water, top up the liquid to 5 litres (5¼ quarts) per 100 g (3½ oz) yarn (dry weight). Leave to cool to 30°C (86°F) – the dye liquid is likely to be hotter than this, despite being topped up with cold water.

3. When the dye liquid is at 30°C (86°F), place the pre-mordanted and dampened yarn into it. Slowly increase the temperature to 80–90°C (176–194°F). Maintaining this temperature, dye for 1 hour.

4. Take the dye bath off the heat source. Leave the yarn in the dyeing liquid to cool to room temperature.

5. Remove the yarn from the dyeing liquid, reserving the dyeing liquid. Rinse the yarn (see page 43) and dry flat.

6. Divide the remaining dye liquid into two equal parts and reserve these as the afterbaths for recipes IV and V (*see right*).

RECIPE IV
CC3 (PURPLE COCHINEAL)

1 portion of reserved cochineal liquid per 100 g (3½ oz) yarn, using 5% of the dry weight of the yarn (5 g/⅙ oz) iron mordant (ferrous sulphate) as a post-mordant

1. Put the reserved cochineal liquid into a dye bath and top up the liquid to 5 litres (5¼ quarts) per 100 g (3½ oz) yarn (dry weight). Heat it to 30°C (86°F), then place the pre-mordanted and dampened yarn in it. Slowly increase the temperature to 80–90°C (176–194°F). Maintaining this temperature, dye for 1 hour.

2. Carefully lift the yarn out of the dye temporarily, mix in the iron mordant, then return the yarn to the dye bath. Maintaining a temperature of 80–90°C (176–194°F), dye for 15 minutes.

3. Remove the yarn from the dye bath. Leave it in a bucket to cool, then rinse (see page 43) and dry flat.

RECIPE V
CC4 (REDDISH YELLOW COCHINEAL)

1 portion of reserved Cochineal liquid per 100 g (3½ oz) yarn, combined with the reserved Reseda afterbath from recipe I

1. Put the combined afterbaths into a dye bath. Heat the liquid to 30°C (86°F.) When the dye liquid is at 30°C (86°F), put the pre-mordanted and dampened yarn into it. Slowly increase the temperature to 80–90°C (176–194°F). Maintaining this temperature, dye for 1 hour.

2. Take the dye bath off the heat. Leave the yarn in the dye liquid to cool overnight. Then remove it from the dye liquid, rinse it (see page 43), and dry flat.

"

The Lempi cardigan is light and warm, and the open neckline won't irritate the sensitive skin around your neck. This pattern can help you reduce stash waste – I used scraps of leftover yarns as well as new balls to make it. This cardigan is knitted flat from the top down. Use garter stitch if you prefer (except for on the button band, neck, and ribbing). If you don't like stripes, why not work an Intarsia pattern instead to really make this great basic cardigan design your own?

Lempi (Favourite)

DESIGNER TIINA KAARELA (PUIKKOMAISTERI)

LEMPI (FAVOURITE)

MODEL SIZE L

Sizes: XS (S, M, L, XL, XXL)

Recommended positive ease 6 cm (2⅜ in).

Dimensions of finished sweater:

Chest circumference: 99 (104, 109, 114, 119, 124) cm (39 (41, 42⅞, 44⅞, 46⅞, 48¾) in).

Length from armpit to hem:
54 cm (21¼ in), or desired length.

Circumference of upper sleeve:
37.5 (39.5, 41.5, 43, 45, 47) cm (14¾ (15½, 16⅜, 17, 17¾, 18½) in).

Wrist circumference: 24 (24, 25, 25, 26.5, 26.5) cm (9½ (9½, 9⅞, 9⅞, 10½, 10½) in).

Inner sleeve length: 42 (42, 43, 43, 44, 44) cm (16½ (16½, 17, 17, 17⅜, 17⅜) in).

Yarn (see conversions on page 11): Ístex Léttlopi (100% wool; 100 m/50 g) or equivalent Aran/Worsted weight yarn.
700–900 g of leftover yarn and individual balls, depending on the size and length of the sweater.

Needles: Circular needles (80 and 100 cm/32 and 40 in) and double-pointed needles in sizes 3.5 mm (US 4) and 5 mm (US 8).

You will also need: Stitch markers, waste yarn or stitch holders, a tapestry needle, and buttons of a suitable size.

Tension (gauge): 16 sts and 26 rows = 10 × 10 cm (4 x 4 in) in stocking (stockinette) stitch on 5 mm needles, lightly blocked.

The pattern does not specify when to change colours. Switch yarns on RS rows based on to the quantities of yarn colours you have or according to your own colourway design.

YOKE

Using 3.5 mm needles, cast on 87 (93, 99, 105, 111, 117) sts.

Row 1 (RS): Slip 1 purlwise, p1, knit until 2 sts remain, p1, k1.

Row 2 (WS): Slip 1 purlwise, k1, purl until 2 sts remain, k2.

Row 3 (RS): Slip 1 purlwise, p1, (k1, p1) 4 times (button band), PM, p12 (13, 14, 15, 16, 17) sts (right front section), PM, p8 (9, 10, 11, 12, 13) sts (right sleeve), PM, p27 (29, 31, 33, 35, 37) sts (back section), PM, p8 (9, 10, 11, 12, 13) sts (left sleeve), PM, p12 (13, 14, 15, 16, 17) (left front section), PM, *p1, k1, repeat from * until the end of the row.

Ribbing (WS): (Slip all markers when you come to them) slip 1 purlwise, k1, *p1, k1, repeat from * until 1 st remains, k1. Work in rib for another 4 rows.

Make the first buttonhole: Make buttonholes on the button band at intervals of 8 cm (3⅛ in) at the end of RS rows as directed below. Note that, for the first buttonhole, to "work in pattern", work in rib as established in ribbing rows 1 (for WS) and 2 (for RS) above. For subsequent buttonholes, you will work in stocking stitch between the button bands to "work in pattern".

Buttonhole row 1 (RS): Work in pattern to last stitch marker, SM, (p1, k1) 2 times, k2tog, (yo) 2 times, k2tog, p1, k1.

Buttonhole row 2 (WS): Slip 1 purlwise, k1, (k1, p1 tbl) over yarnovers, **p1, k1, repeat from ** to next stitch marker, work in pattern to end.

If you wish to change colour when it is time to make a buttonhole, ensure you do so on buttonhole row 1, as colour should be changed on a RS row).

After completing buttonhole rows 1 and 2, continue in rib as established in ribbing rows 1 and 2 for another 4 rows.

Work the short rows for the neck: Switch to 5 mm needles. From this point until the hem ribbing, work in stocking stitch but work the button band in rib as established in the ribbing rows (except buttonhole rows). Below, this is referred to as "work button band".

Row 1 (RS): Work button band, SM, (knit to 1 st before next stitch marker, M1R, k1, SM, M1L) 4 times, k4, turn.

Row 2 (WS): Make a DS, (purl to next stitch marker, SM) 4 times, p6, turn work.

Row 3: Make a DS, (knit to 1 st before next stitch marker, M1R, k1, MM, M1L) 4 times, knit to DS, knit the DS as a single stitch, k3, turn work.

Row 4: Make a DS, purl to DS, purl DS as a single st, p3, turn work.

Repeat rows 3 and 4 one more time.

Row 7: Make a DS, (knit to 1 st before next stitch marker, M1R, k1, MM, M1L) 4 times, knit to DS, knit DS as a single stitch, knit to final stitch marker, turn work.

Row 8: Make a DS, purl to DS, purl DS as a single stitch, purl to final stitch marker, turn work.

Row 9: Make a DS, (knit to 1 st before next stitch marker, M1R, k1, MM, M1L) 4 times, knit to DS, knit DS as a single stitch, k3, SM, work button band.

Row 10: Work button band SM, purl to DS, purl DS as a single stitch, SM, work button band.

Work the raglan increases: These are worked on every second row as follows:

Row 1 (RS): Work button band, SM, (knit to 1 st before next stitch marker, M1R, k1, MM, M1L) 4 times, knit to next stitch marker, SM, work button band.

Row 2 (WS): Work button band, SM, (purl to next stitch marker, SM) 5 times, work button band.

Repeat rows 1 and 2 another 16 (17, 17, 18, 19, 19) times. You have 10 sts on each button band, 34 (36, 37, 39, 41, 42) sts on each front section, 52 (55, 56, 59, 62, 63) sts on each sleeve, and 71 (75, 77, 81, 85, 87) sts on the back section. [263 (277, 283, 297, 311, 317) sts in total] Continue working in stocking stitch, working the button bands as established, until the depth of the yoke measures 21 (23, 25, 27, 29, 31) cm (8¼ (9, 9⅞, 10⅝, 11½, 12¼) in) from the start of the work.

Separate the body and sleeves:

Next row (RS): Work button band, SM, knit to stitch marker, RM, transfer 52 (55, 56, 59, 62, 63) right sleeve stitches to waste yarn, cast on 4 (4, 5, 5, 5, 6) sts, PM, cast on 4 (4, 5, 5, 5, 6) sts, RM, knit to stitch marker, RM, transfer 52 (55, 56, 59, 62, 63) left sleeve stitches to waste yarn, cast on 4 (4, 5, 5, 5, 6) sts, PM, cast on 4 (4, 5, 5, 5, 6) sts, RM, knit to stitch marker, MM, work button band. You should now have 175 (183, 191, 199, 207, 215) body stitches.

BODY

Continue working in stocking stitch, working the button bands as established, for another 6 rows.

Work the side increases/set up the pocket holes:

*Increase row: Work button band, SM, (knit to 1 st before the next stitch marker, M1R, k1, SM, k1, M1L) 2 times, knit to stitch marker, SM, work button band. Continue working in stocking stitch, working the button bands as established, for a further 7 rows.** Repeat from * to ** a further 7 times OR until you achieve a suitable width (if you are making a max-length cardigan, for example – continue the increases until at least the hip). You should now have 207 (215, 223, 231, 239, 247) sts.

Once the length of the work measures 38 cm (15 in) from the armpit, make the holes for the pockets on the next RS row as follows: work button band, SM, knit until there are 28 (30, 31, 32, 34, 34) sts remaining before the next stitch marker, use a piece of waste yarn to knit the next 20 (20, 21, 22, 23, 23) sts, then transfer those stitches back onto the left needle and knit them again, SM, knit to stitch marker, SM, k8 (10, 10, 10, 11, 11) sts, use a piece of waste yarn to knit the next 20 (20, 21, 22, 23, 23) sts, then transfer those stitches back onto the left needle and knit them again, knit to stitch marker, SM, work button band. Continue working in stocking stitch, working the button bands as established, until the cardigan has

reached your desired length (work at least 18 cm (7 in) after the waste yarn so the base of the pocket does not overshoot the hem in the finished piece).
Ribbing: Switch to 3.5 mm needles. Work 10 rows of (k1, p1) ribbing. Cast (bind) off loosely.

SLEEVES

Beginning at the centre of the stitches you cast on on the body for the armpit, pick up and knit 4 (4, 5, 5, 5, 6) sts, knit the reserved 52 (55, 56, 59, 62, 63) sleeve stitches, then pick up and knit another 4 (4, 5, 5, 5, 6) sts from the armpit on the body, PM. You should now have 60 (63, 66, 69, 72, 75) sts.

Work in the round in stocking stitch until the length of the sleeve from the armpit is 17 (17, 17, 17, 15, 15) cm (6½ (6½, 6½, 6½, 6, 6) in).

Work the sleeve decreases:

Decrease row: K1, k2tog and knit until 3 stitches remain, ssk, k1.

Continue working in the round in stocking stitch, repeating this decrease row every 6th (6th, 5th, 5th, 5th, 5th) round, until the length of the sleeve from the armpit measures 38 (38, 39, 39, 40, 40) cm (15 (15, 15⅜, 15⅜, 15¾, 15¾) in) (or desired length). On the last row, decrease at even intervals so that 38 (38, 40, 40, 42, 42) sts remain.

Ribbing: Switch to 3.5 mm needles. Work 10 rows of (k1, p1) ribbing. Cast off loosely.

POCKETS

Pick up stitches from above and below the waste yarn, removing it as you go, and knit in the round on larger needles until the pocket measures 16 cm (6¼ in) deep. Graft the bottom of the pocket closed.

FINISHING

Sew the ends into the wrong side of the work, sew on buttons, and steam the cardigan or wash it in a solution of mild wool detergent and let dry.

> I knitted two Lempi cardigans using the same pattern but varying the height of the stripes: I knitted one cardigan from different waste yarns with a two-row stripe, and in the other, the stripes were 20 rows high. In the latter, the individual balls of yarn ran out in the sleeves, so I made two layers of stripes there, too. The cardigans were wonderfully different!

"

Nuppunen uses Finnsheep wool, which has a softness that lends itself well to children's clothes. The front and back of the sweater are identical, which makes it easier for a child to put on (there's no wrong way around!) but, if you wish, you can shape the back of the neck using short rows. The sweater is knitted from the top down, so that, by frogging the ribbing and knitting more length into the sleeves and front, you allow the young wearer to use it for longer as they grow.

Nuppunen (Little Bud)

DESIGNER MINTTU WIKBERG

NUPPUNEN (LITTLE BUD)

MODEL SHOWN IS SIZE 100 CM

Sizes (height): 100 (120, 140, 160) cm
(39⅜ (47¼, 55⅛, 63) in)
Recommended positive ease approx. 12 cm (4¾ in).

Dimensions of finished sweater:
Chest circumference: 69 (75.5, 84.5, 93.5) cm
(27⅛ (29¾, 33¼, 36¾) in).
Length from armpit to hem: 25 (29, 33, 38) cm
(9⅞ (11½, 13, 15) in).
Length from front collar to hem: 40 (45, 51, 57) cm
(15¾ (17¾, 20⅛, 22½) in).
Circumference of upper sleeve: 26.5 (28, 32, 34.5) cm
(10½ (11, 12⅝, 13⅝) in).
Wrist circumference: 18 (18, 20, 22) cm (7 (7, 7⅞, 8⅝) in).
Inner sleeve length: 30 (35, 42, 51) cm
(11¾ (13¾, 16½, 20⅛) in).

Yarn (see conversions on page 11): Kaarama Tenho
(100% wool; 100 m/50 g) or equivalent Aran/
Worsted weight yarn.
MC: Honka 4 (6, 7, 8) skeins or 330 (600, 700, 800) m
CC1: Luonnonvalkoinen 1 (1, 1, 2) skein(s) or
65 (80, 100, 125) m
CC2: Sarastus 1 (1, 1, 1) skein or 35 (50, 65, 80) m
CC3: Olki 1 (1, 1, 1) skein or 10 (30, 40, 50) m

Needles: Circular needles (80 and 100 cm/32 and
40 in) and double-pointed needles in sizes 3.5 mm
(US 4) and 4 mm (US 6). If necessary, 4.5 mm (US 7)
circular needles for the stranded knitting section.

You will also need: Stitch markers, waste yarn
or stitch holders, and a tapestry needle.

Tension (gauge):
18 sts and 25 rows = 10 × 10 cm
(4 x 4 in) in stocking (stockinette) stitch,
lightly blocked.

MC
CC1
CC2
CC3
M1L

chart a

2 1

chart b
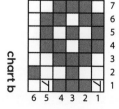
6 5 4 3 2 1

chart c
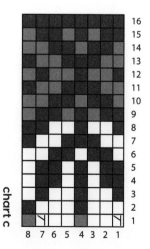
8 7 6 5 4 3 2 1

YOKE

Using 3.5 mm needles and CC3, cast on 78 (84, 86, 90) sts. Join work in the round, ensuring not to twist the row of sts. PM.

Ribbing: Switch to CC1. *K1, p1, repeat from * to end. Repeat this round until ribbing measures 2.5 (2.5, 3, 3) cm (1 (1, 1¼, 1¼) in).

Next round: Switch to 4 mm needles. *K1 in CC2, k1 in CC1, repeat from * to end. Break CC2.

Increase round: Using CC1, work an increase round as follows:

Size 100 only: K1, (k5, M1L, k6, M1L) 7 times. [14 sts increased – 92 sts in total]

Size 120 only: *(K5, M1L) 3 times, k6, M1L, repeat from * to end. [16 sts increased – 100 sts in total]

Size 140 only: K1, M1L, (k3, M1L, k4, M1L) 12 times, k1, M1L. [26 sts increased – 112 sts in total]

Size 160 only: K5, M1L, (k3, M1L, k2, M1L) 16 times, k5, M1L. [34 sts increased – 124 sts in total]

(All sizes) If you are not working short rows for the neck:

Using CC1, continue in stocking stitch for 1 (2, 3, 4) rounds before following chart A.

(All sizes) If you are working short rows for the neck:

For a raised neck, work the following short rows. Each time you reach a DS made previously, remember to knit it as a single stitch.

Row 1 (RS): K27 (30, 33, 37) sts, turn work.

Row 2 (WS): Make a DS, purl to the round marker, turn work.

Row 3 (RS): Make a DS, k42 (46, 50, 55) sts (knit the DS as a single stitch), turn work.

Row 4 (WS): Make a DS, p57 (62, 67, 73) sts. Turn the work.

Row 5 (RS): Make a DS and knit to the round marker (knitting each DS as a single stitch).

Follow chart A: Using CC1 and CC2, work the rows of the chart. The pattern repeats 46 (50, 56, 62) times per round.

Follow chart B: Using CCs 1, 2, and 3, work the rows of the chart, making increases on round 1 as indicated. The pattern repeats 23 (25, 28, 31) times per round. [46 (50, 56, 62) sts increased – 138 (150, 168, 186) sts in total]

Follow chart C: Using MC and CCs 1, 2, and 3, work the rows of the chart, making increases on round 1 as indicated. The pattern repeats 23 (25, 28, 31) times per round. After completing the chart, cut all CC yarns. [46 (50, 56, 62) sts increased – 184 (200, 224, 248) sts in total]

Complete the yoke: Using MC, continue working in the round in stocking stitch until yoke measures at least 15 (16, 18, 19) cm (6 (6¼, 7, 7½) in) from cast-on edge.

Separate the sleeves: K54 (60, 66, 74) sts for the back, then transfer the next 38 (40, 46, 50) sts onto waste yarn for the right sleeve. Cast on 8 (8, 10, 10) sts for the right armpit directly after the stitches you just knitted for the back. K54 (60, 66, 74) sts for the front, then transfer the next 38 (40, 46, 50) sts onto waste yarn for the left sleeve. Now cast on 8 (8, 10, 10) sts for the left armpit directly after the stitches you just knitted for the front.

BODY

The body now has 124 (136, 152, 168) sts. Using MC and working in stocking stitch, continue to work in the round until the length of the work from the armpit measures 20 (24, 28, 33) cm (7⅞ (9½, 11, 13) in).

Next round: *K1 in CC2, k1 in MC, repeat from * to end of the round. Cut CC2.

Ribbing: Switch to 3.5 mm needles. In MC, *k1, p1, repeat from * to end.

Repeat this round until ribbing measures 5 cm (2 in). Cast (bind) off in rib.

SLEEVES

Transfer the 38 (40, 46, 50) sts for one sleeve from waste yarn onto 4 mm circular needles. Using MC, pick up 8 (8, 10, 10) sts from the stitches cast on for the armpit, pick up 1 st from both sides of the divide between the armpit stitches and yoke to prevent holes. You should now have 48 (50, 58, 62) sts. Join in the round and place a stitch marker in the centre armpit, at the midway point of the new sts you just picked up. Knit in stocking stitch until the length of the work from the armpit measures 3 (1, 1, 3) cm (1¼ (⅜, ⅜, 1¼) in).

Work the sleeve decreases: Decreases are made on both sides of the round marker. Each pair of decrease rounds decreases the stitch count by 2.

Decrease round 1: Knit to 2 sts before the round marker, k2tog tbl.

Decrease round 2: K2tog, knit to end.

Continue working in the round in stocking stitch, repeating these two decrease rounds once every 3 (3.5, 3.5, 4) cm (1¼ (1⅜, 1⅜, 1½) in) a further 7 (8, 10, 10) times. You should now have 32 (32, 36, 40) sts.

Complete the sleeve: Continue working in the round in stocking stitch until the length of the sleeve from the armpit is 26 (30, 37, 46) cm (10¼, (11¾, 14½, 18⅛) in).

Next round: *K1 in CC2, k1 in MC, repeat from to end.

Ribbing: Switch to 3.5 mm needles. In MC, *k1, p1, repeat from * to end.

Repeat this round until ribbing measures 4 (5, 5, 5) cm (1½ (2, 2, 2 in). Cast off in rib.

FINISHING

Sew in the ends on the wrong side of the work. Carefully dampen the work (try using a spray bottle). Shape the sweater, then lay flat to dry. Fluffy yarn felts easily, so wash the sweater gently by hand. Most often, airing and careful stain removal is enough for wool.

I named Hillasuo once I saw the finished sweater and its vibrant colours, which remind me of the hues of a swamp bejewelled with beautiful cloudberries. But, of course, the pattern takes on an entirely different feel if you choose other colours. The pattern is perhaps more traditionally Icelandic knitting than anything else in this book. Hillasuo is knitted from the bottom up.

Hillasuo (Cloudberry swamp)

DESIGNER MERJA OJANPERÄ

HILLASUO (CLOUDBERRY SWAMP)

MODEL SHOWN IS SIZE S

Sizes: S (M, L)
Recommended ease approx. 5 cm (2 in).

Dimensions of finished sweater:
Chest circumference: 99 (103.5, 108) cm
(39 (40¾, 42½) in).
Length from armpit to hem: 44 (45, 46) cm
(17¾ (17¾, 18⅛) in).
Length from front collar to hem:
73 (74, 76) cm (28¾ (29⅛, 29⅞) in).
Circumference of upper sleeve: 37.5
(40, 44.5) cm (14¾ (15¾, 17½) in).
Wrist circumference: 23.5 (26, 28) cm
(9¼ (10¼, 11) in).
Inner sleeve length: 44 (45, 47) cm
(17⅜ (17¾, 18½) in).

Yarn (see conversions on page 11): Novita
Icelandic Wool (100% wool; 90 m/50 g) or
equivalent Aran/Worsted weight yarn.
MC: 638 Seitikki 8 (8, 9) balls or
650 (720, 795) m
CC1: 164 Mustikka 1 (2, 2) ball(s) or 85 (95, 105) m
CC2: 663 Tatti 1 (1, 2) ball(s) or 75 (85, 95) m
CC3: 010 Luonnonvalkoinen 2 (2, 3) balls or
165 (180, 200) m

Needles: Circular needles (40 and 80 cm/16
and 32 in) and double-pointed needles in size
4.5 mm (US 7).

You will also need: Stitch markers, waste yarn
or stitch holders, and a tapestry needle.

Tension (gauge): 17 sts and 20 rows = 10 ×
10 cm (4 x 4 in) in stocking (stockinette) stitch,
lightly blocked.

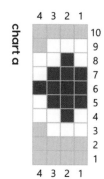

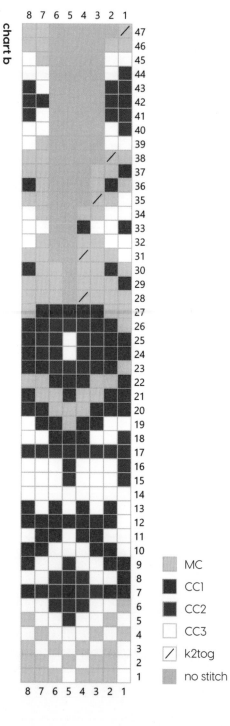

SLEEVES

Using MC, cast on 40 (44, 48) sts. Join in the round, being careful not to twist the row of stitches. PM. Working in stocking stitch, work 5 rounds.

Ribbing: K1 tbl, p1* repeat from * to end.
Repeat previous round 9 more times. On the last round of ribbing, increase 4 (4, 4) sts at even intervals. You should now have 44 (48, 52) sts.

Follow chart A: Using MC and CCs 1, 2, and 3, work the rows of the chart. The pattern repeats 11 (12. 13) times per round. When you have completed all 10 rows of chart A, cut the CCs.

Work the sleeve increases: *Using MC, k1, M1L, knit to 1 st before round marker, M1R, k1.
Work in stocking stitch for 6 rounds.**
Repeat from * to ** a further 9 (9, 11) times. You should now have 64 (68, 76) sts.

Complete the sleeve: Continue working in the round in stocking stitch until the sleeve measures 44 (45, 47) cm (17⅜ (17¾, 18½) in) from the cast-on edge (or a suitable length from the cast-on edge to the armpit).

Next round: Knit to last 5 (5, 6) sts. Transfer the next 10 (10, 12) sts (5 (5, 6) stitches from either side of the round marker) to waste yarn, RM.
Set aside the remaining 54 (58, 64) sleeve stitches and knit the other sleeve in the same way.

BODY

Using MC, cast on 168 (176, 184) sts. Join in the round, being careful not to twist the row of stitches. PM (this is positioned at the left side), and another after 84 (88, 92) sts (as a side marker).

Ribbing: *K1 tbl, p1, repeat from * to end.
Repeat this round 9 more times.

Follow chart A: Using MC and CCs 1, 2, and 3, work the rows of the chart. The pattern repeats 42 (44, 46) times per round. When you have completed all 10 rows of the chart, cut the CCs.

Using MC, continue working in the round in stocking stitch until the work measures 44 (45, 46) cm (17⅜ (17¾, 18¼) in) from hem to armpit.

YOKE

Join the body and sleeves: Knit to 5 (5, 6) sts before side marker. Move next 10 (10, 12) sts onto waste yarn (remove side marker). PM (this is the new round marker), transfer the 54 (58, 64) sleeve stitches for one sleeve from the waste yarn onto your needles and knit them. Next, knit the body stitches to 5 (5, 6) sts before the marker. Transfer the next 10 (10, 12) sts to waste yarn (remove the side marker), transfer the 54 (58, 64) sts for the remaining sleeve to your needles and knit to round marker. You should now have 256 (272, 288) sts. The start of the round is now at the seam between the back section and left sleeve.

Follow chart B: Using MC and CCs 1, 2, and 3, work the rows of the chart, making decreases as indicated. The pattern repeats 32 (34, 36) times. When you have completed all 47 rows of the chart, cut the CCs. You should now have 96 (102, 108) sts. If necessary, continue knitting rounds in stocking stitch in MC until the yoke is the desired depth.

NECK

Using MC, work 1 round, decreasing 10 (12, 14) sts at even intervals. You should now have 86 (90, 94) sts.

Ribbing: *K1 tbl, p1, repeat from * to end.
Repeat this round 5 more times.
Work in stocking stitch for 5 (5, 7) rounds.
Cast (bind) off using a stretchy cast-off method.

FINISHING

Sew all the ends into the wrong side of the work. Graft the armpit stitches. Wet the sweater and then squeeze dry. Shape and lay flat to dry.

"

My friend Kalle was an enthusiastic cyclist even before the recent boom in cycling caused by climate change. Die-hard cyclists cool off in technical textiles and use high-visibility vests or other reflective cycling shirts, but for a more laid-back cycle to work or into town, or for an enjoyable cycle in the countryside, a woollen sweater is a great way to warm up – plus, airing the sweater after activity freshens it up, so any perspiration odours will be gone in no time.

Kalle

DESIGNER TIINA KAARELA (PUIKKOMAISTERI)

KALLE

Sizes: XS (S, M, L, XL, XXL)

Recommended ease 6 cm (2⅜ in).

Dimensions of finished sweater:

Chest circumference: 89 (93.5, 100, 102, 108, 111) cm (35 (36¾, 39⅜, 40⅛, 42½, 43¾) in).

Length from armpit to hem: 40 (42, 44, 46, 48, 48) cm (15¾ (16½, 17⅜, 18⅛, 18⅞, 18⅞) in).

Length from front collar to hem: 64 (66, 69.5, 71.5, 74, 74.5) cm (25¼ (26, 27⅜, 28⅛, 29⅛, 29¼) in).

Circumference of upper sleeve: 36.5 (38, 39, 40, 41, 42) cm (14⅜ (15, 15⅜, 15¾, 16⅛, 16½) in).

Wrist circumference: 22 (22, 24.5, 24.5, 26.5, 26.5) cm (8⅝ (8⅝, 9⅝, 9⅝, 10½, 10½) in).

Inner sleeve length: 47 (49, 50, 51, 52, 53) cm (18½ (19¼, 19⅝, 20⅛, 20½, 20⅞) in).

Yarn (see conversions on page 11): Novita Icelandic Wool (100% wool; 90 m/50 g) or equivalent Aran/Worsted weight yarn

MC: 045 Savi 6 (7, 8, 9, 9, 10) balls or 540 (630, 720, 810, 810, 900) m

CC1: 384 Mänty 1 (1, 2, 2, 2, 3) ball or 90 (90, 180, 180, 180, 270) m

CC2: 638 Seitikki 1 (1, 1, 2, 2, 2) ball or 90 (90, 90, 180, 180, 180) m

CC3: 601 Jyvä 1 (1, 1, 1, 1, 1) ball or 90 (90, 90, 90, 90, 90) m

CC4: 523 Puolukka 1 (1, 1, 1, 1, 1) ball or 90 (90, 90, 90, 90, 90) m

---

Needles: Circular needles (80 and 100 cm/32 and 40 in) and double-pointed needles in sizes 5 mm (US 8) and 3.5 mm (US 4).

You will also need: Stitch markers, waste yarn or stitch holders, and a tapestry needle.

Tension (gauge): 18 sts and 24 rows = 10 × 10 cm (4 x 4 in) in stocking (stockinette) stitch on 5 mm needles, lightly blocked.

BODY

Using 3.5 mm needles and MC, cast on 160 (168, 180, 184, 192, 200) sts. Do not join in the round.

Ribbing: *K2, p2, repeat from * to end.

Repeat this row a further 9 times.

Join in the round, ensuring not to twist the work. PM. Knit 2 more rounds of ribbing. **Size XL only:** on final round, increase 2 sts at regular intervals.

Switch to 5 mm needles. Continue in stocking stitch until the work measures 40 (42, 44, 46, 48, 48) cm (15¾ (16½, 17⅜, 18⅛, 18⅞, 19) in) from cast-on edge. Transfer sts to waste yarn and set aside. Do not cut the yarn.

SLEEVES

Using 3.5 mm needles and MC, cast on 40 (40, 44, 44, 48, 48) sts. Do not join in the round.

Ribbing: *K2, p2, repeat from * to end.

Repeat this row a further 9 times.

Join in the round, ensuring not to twist the stitches. PM. Work 2 more rounds of ribbing.

Work the sleeve increases: Switch to 5 mm needles.

Increase round: K1, M1L, knit to final st, M1R, k1. *[2 sts increased]*

Continue working in stocking stitch, repeating the increase round once every 7th (7th, 8th, 7th, 8th, 8th) round a further 12 (13, 12, 13, 12, 13) times. You should now have 66 (68, 70, 72, 74, 76) sts.

Complete the sleeve: Continue working in stocking stitch until sleeve measures 47 (49, 50, 51, 52, 53) cm (18½ (19¼, 19⅝, 20⅛, 20½, 20⅞) in) from cast-on edge. For the left sleeve, slip the first 9 (10, 11, 12, 13, 14) of the round onto waste yarn and set aside. Work the right sleeve in the same way, but at the end, slip the last 9 (10, 11, 12, 13, 14) of the round onto waste yarn.

YOKE

Join the body and sleeves: Using 5 mm needles and MC, RM, k71 (74, 79, 80, 84, 86) sts from the body for the back section, PM (this is new round marker),

transfer the next 9 (10, 11, 12, 13, 14) sts to waste yarn, k57 (58, 59, 60, 61, 62) sts reserved for the left sleeve, PM, k71 (74, 79, 80, 84, 86) sts from the body for the front section, PM, transfer the next 9 (10, 11, 12, 13, 14) sts onto waste yarn, k57 (58, 59, 60, 61, 62) sts reserved for the right sleeve, PM, knit to round marker. You should now have 256 (264, 276, 280, 290, 296) sts.

Follow charts A and B: You will follow both charts simultaneously as directed below. Ensure you use the correct 2 charts for your size (*see pages 80–86*).

Next round: Using MC and CCs 1, 2, 3, and 4, work the stitches for the left sleeve following row 1 of chart A, SM, work the front section following row 1 of chart B, SM, work the right sleeve following row 1 of chart A, SM, work the back section following chart B row 1 of chart B.

Work subsequent chart rows in the same way to complete the yoke design. Note that the decreases do not always occur at equal intervals, neither will the horizontal stripes running across the pattern above the cyclist always align where the sleeves and front/back sections meet. You should have 92 (100, 112, 114, 114, 114) sts. Cut all the CCs.

Decrease round: Using MC, work 1 round, decreasing 24 (28, 36, 38, 36, 34) sts at even intervals. You will now have 72 (72, 76, 76, 80, 80) sts.

NECK

Ribbing: Switch to 3.5 mm needles. *K2, p2, repeat from * to end.

Repeat this round a further 9 times. Cast (bind) off loosely.

FINISHING

Sew in ends. Graft armpit stitches together and seam cuffs and hem. Wash the sweater on a handwash programme (first test with a sample swatch) or by hand, then shape it. Lay flat to dry. It will adapt to the shape of the body during use.

chart a, sizes XS-M

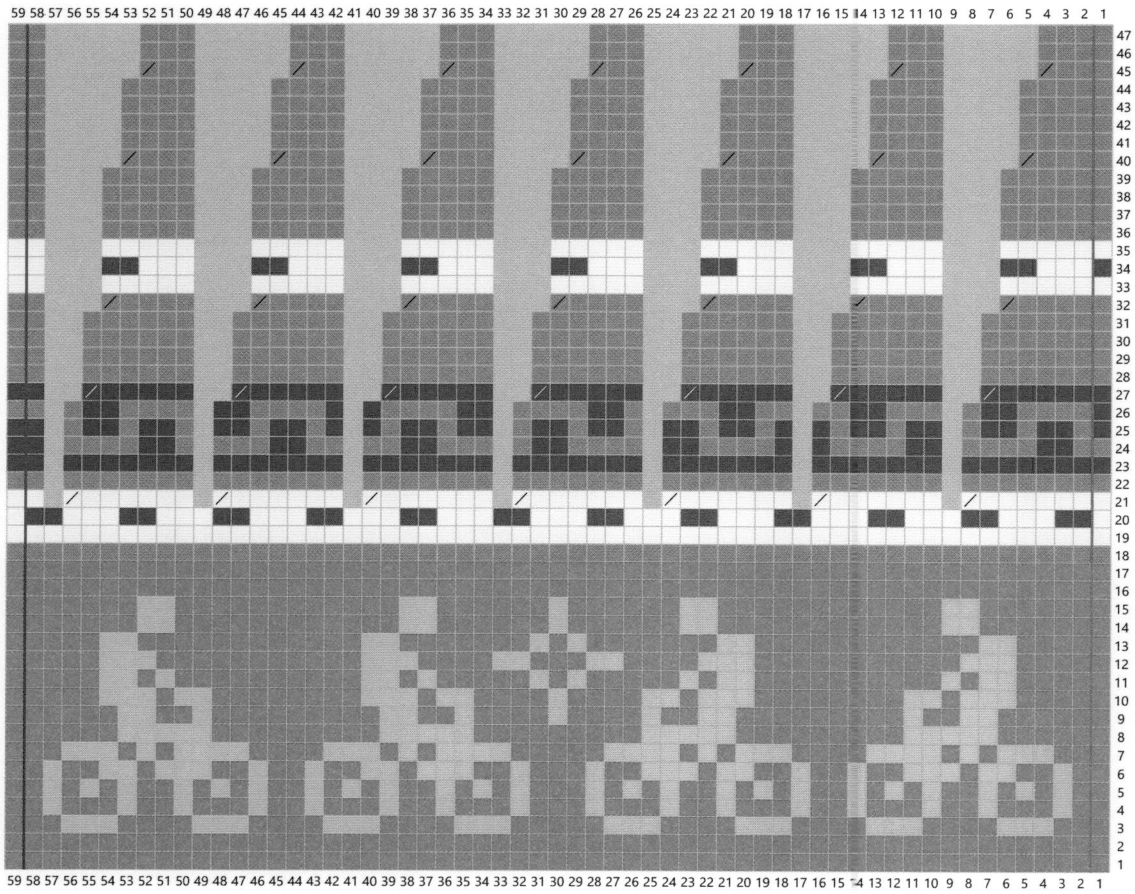

Legend:
- MC
- CC1
- CC2
- CC3
- CC4
- no stitch
- k2tog
- sizes XS and S
- size XS:

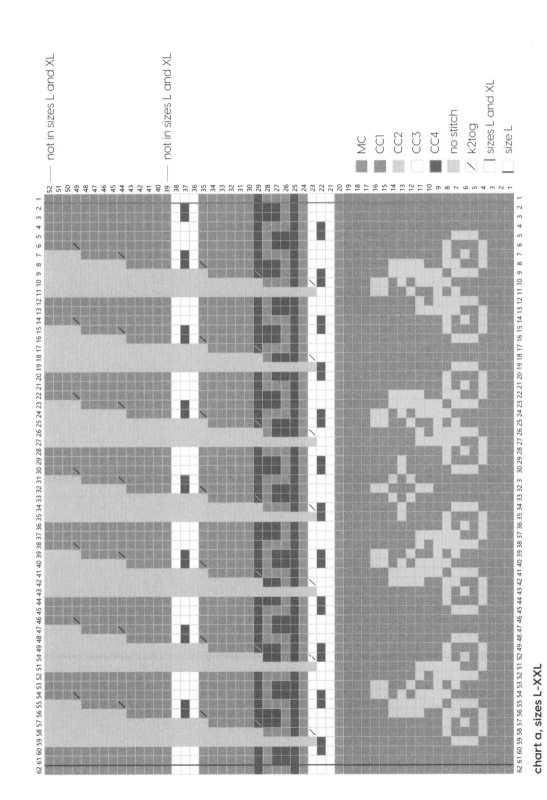

not in sizes L and XL

not in sizes L and XL

MC
CC1
CC2
CC3
CC4
no stitch
k2tog
sizes L and XL
size L

chart a, sizes L–XXL

Chart b, sizes XS-S

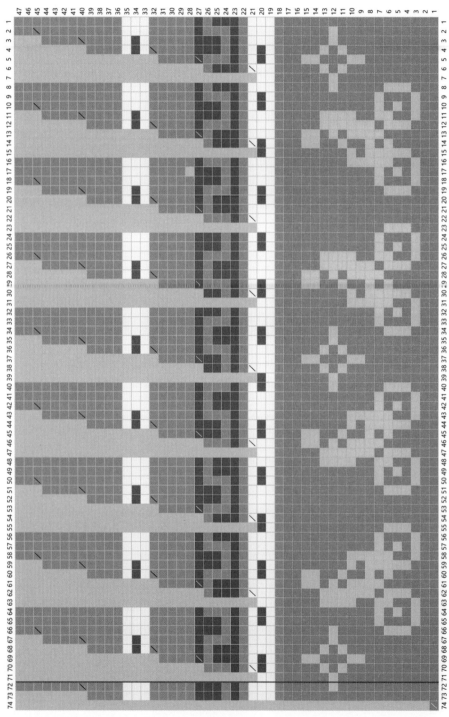

MC
CC1
CC2
CC3
CC4
no stitch
/ k2tog
size XS

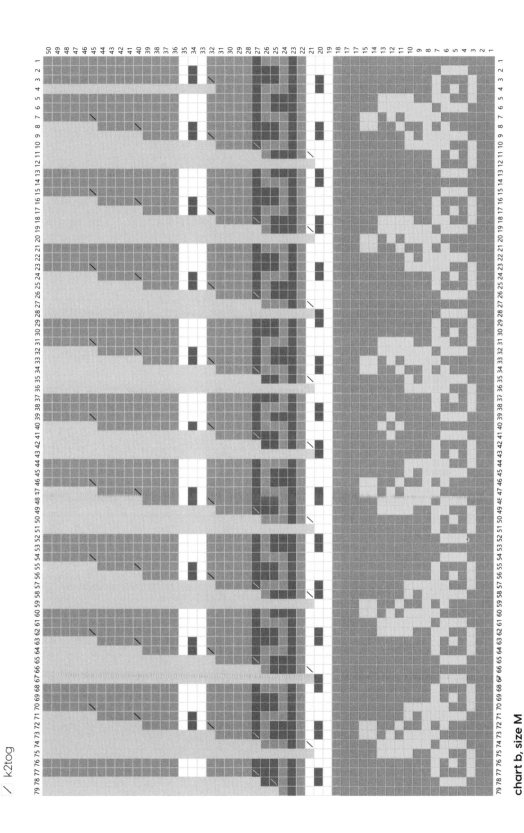

chart b, size M

MC
CC1
CC2
CC3
CC4
no stitch
/ k2tog

chart b, size L

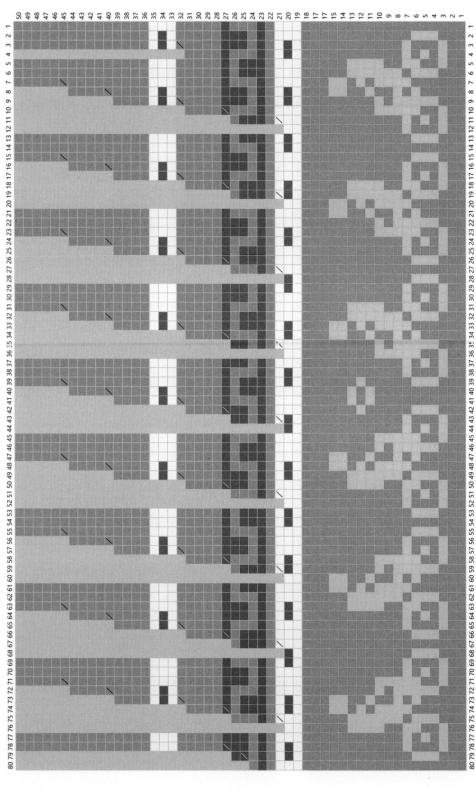

MC
CC1
CC2
CC3
CC4
no stitch
k2tog

84

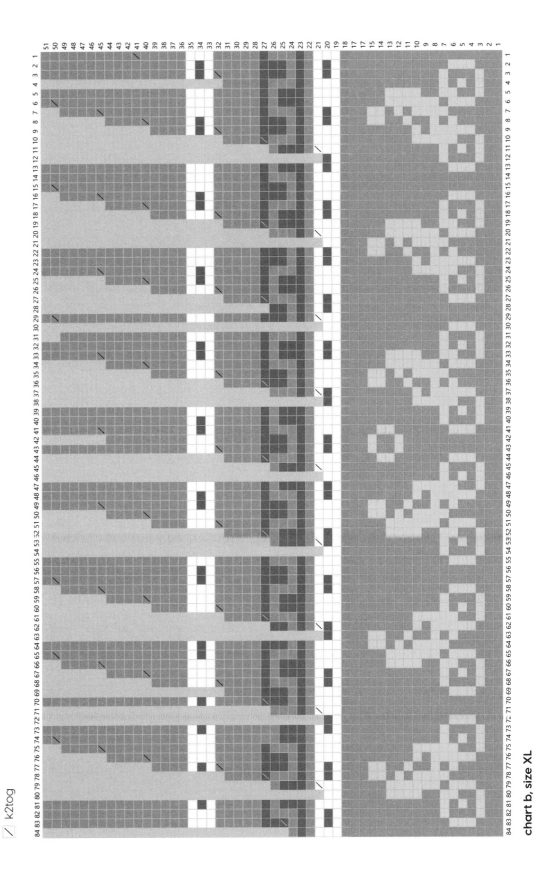

chart b, size XL

chart b, size XXL

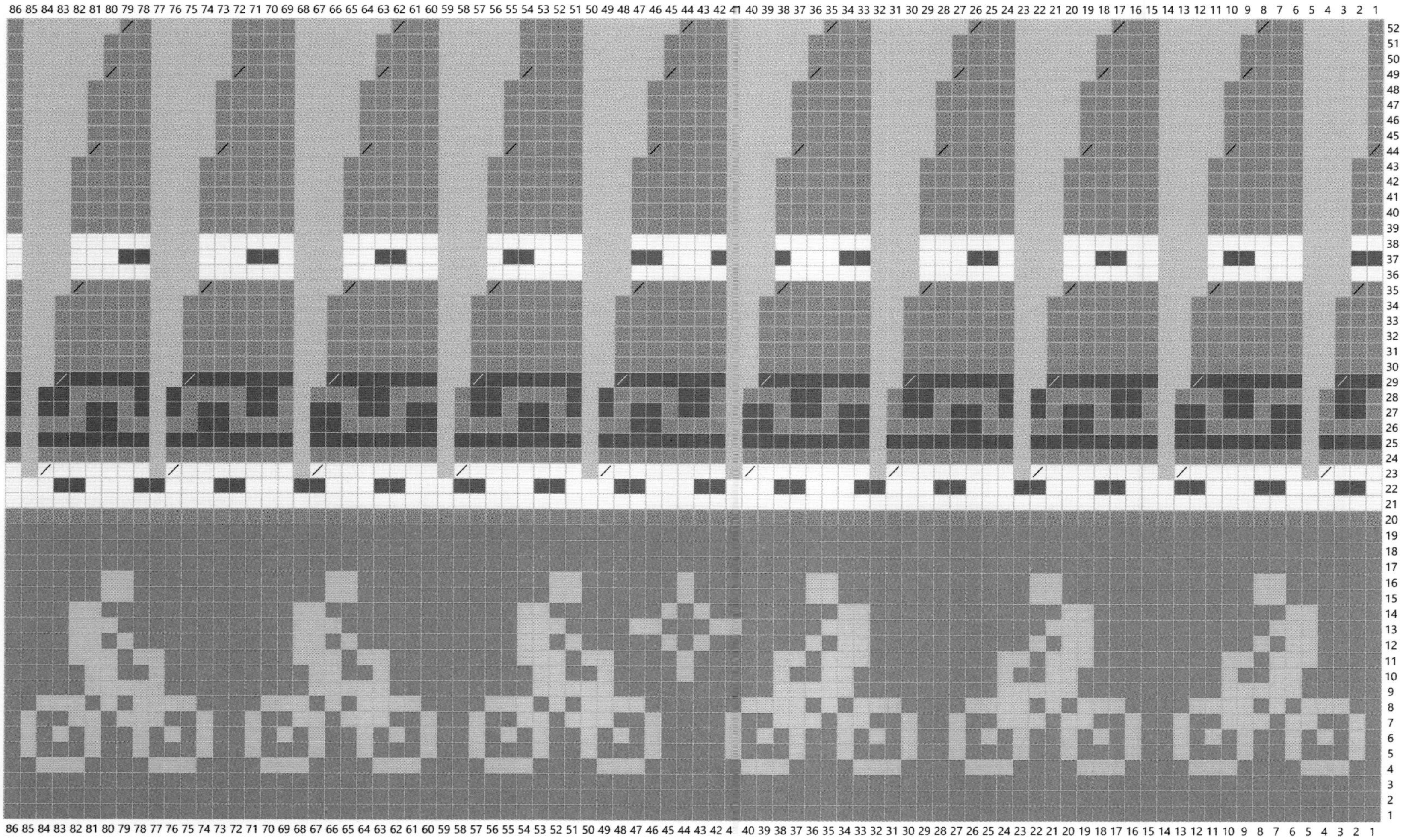

MC
CC1
CC2
CC3
CC4
no stitch
k2tog

86

The best thing about Kalle is its simplicity – there's no need to shape the neck or body at all. You just knit away.

Lapinvuokko, known in English as the white dryas, is a flowering plant that creeps along the ground, and the inspiration for the sweater. Though rare in Finland, the white dryas is the national plant of Iceland. The body of this sweater is knitted from the bottom up, as are the sleeves. The sections are joined at the start of the yoke.

Lapinvuokko (White Dryas)

DESIGNER MERJA OJANPERÄ

LAPINVUOKKO (WHITE DRYAS)

MODEL SHOWN IS SIZE S

Sizes: S (M, L)

Recommended positive ease approx. 5 cm (2 in).

Dimensions of finished sweater:

Chest circumference: 96.5 (106, 113) cm (38 (41¾, 44½) in).

Length from armpit to hem: 48 (49, 50) cm (18⅞ (19¼, 19⅝) in).

Length from front collar to hem: 72 (73, 74) cm (28⅜, (28¾, 29⅛) in).

Circumference of upper sleeve: 39.5 (42, 44) cm (15½ (16½, 17⅜) in).

Wrist circumference: 26 cm (10¼ in).

Inner sleeve length: 47 (48, 50) cm (18½ (18⅞, 19⅝) in).

Yarn (see conversions on page 11): Novita Icelandic Wool (100% wool; 90 m/50 g) or equivalent Aran/Worsted weight yarn.

MC: 045 Savi 7 (9, 10) balls or 630 (730, 850) m

CC1: 384 Mänty 2 (2, 2) balls or 110 (130, 150) m

CC2: 550 Pioni 1 (1, 1) ball or 40 (60, 80) m

CC3: 010 Luonnonvalkoinen 2 (2, 2) balls or 110 (130, 150) m

Needles: Circular needles (40 and 80 cm/16 and 32 in) and double-pointed needles in size 4.5 mm (US 7).

You will also need: Stitch markers, waste yarn or stitch holders, and a tapestry needle.

Tension (gauge): 17 sts and 21 rows = 10 ×10 cm (4 x 4 in) in stocking (stockinette) stitch, lightly blocked.

- MC
- CC1
- CC2
- CC3
- no stitch
- ╱ k2tog
- ⋀ cdd

chart A

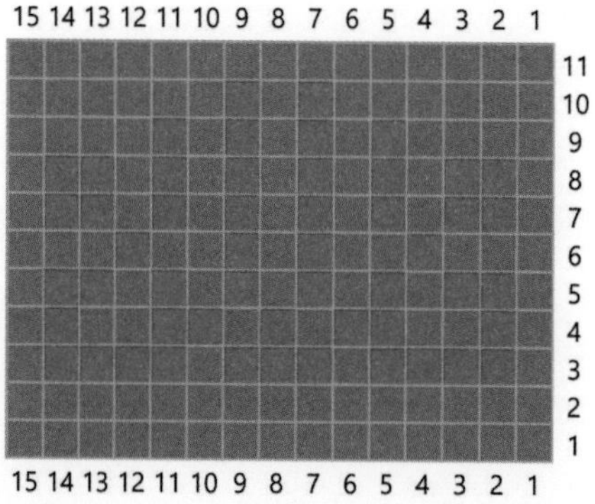

chart B

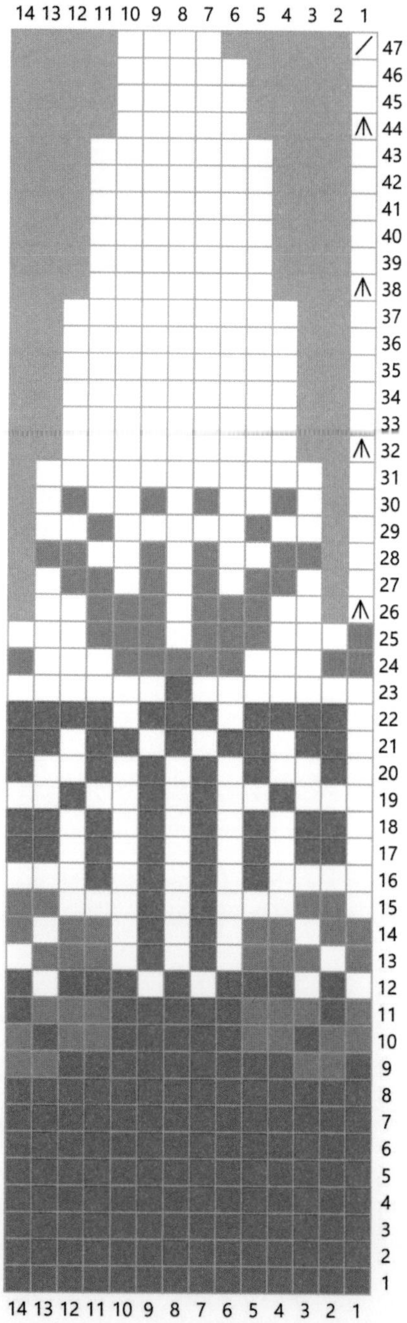

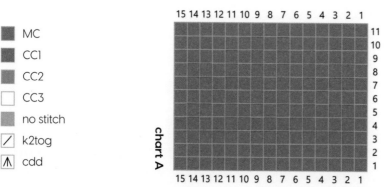

BODY

Using MC, cast on 164 (180, 192) sts. Join in the round, being careful not to twist the work. PM as a round marker, and PM again after 82 (90, 96) sts as a side marker.

Ribbing: *K2, p2, repeat from * to end.

Repeat this round a further 9 times. On the final round, make 1 (0, 3) increase(s). You should now have 165 (180, 195) sts.

Follow chart A: Using MC and CC1, work the rows of the chart. The pattern repeats 11 (12, 13) times. On the last round, decrease 1 (0, 3) sts. You should now have 164 (180, 192) sts.

Continue working in the round in stocking stitch until the sleeve measures 48 (49, 50) cm (18⅞ (19¼, 19⅝) from cast-on edge to armpit OR your desired length. Set aside the body stitches and knit the sleeves

SLEEVES

Using MC, cast on 44 sts. Join in the round, being careful not to twist the work. PM. (This is positioned at the inner sleeve.)

Ribbing: *K2, p2, repeat from * to end.

Repeat this round a further 9 times. On the final round, increase 1 st. You should have 45 sts.

Follow chart A/work sleeve increases: Using MC and CC1, work the rows of the chart. On the last row of the chart, increase as follows:

Increase round: *K1, M1L, knit to final st, M1R, k1. Knit 5 (4, 4) rounds.**

Repeat from * to ** a further 10 (12, 14) times. You should now have 67 (71, 75) sts.

Complete the sleeve: Continue working in the round in stocking stitch until sleeve measures 47 (48, 50) cm (18½ (18⅞, 19⅝ in) OR your desired length from wrist to armpit.

Next round: Knit to last 5 (5, 6) sts. Transfer the next 10 (10, 12) sts to waste yarn (5 (5, 6) sts from either side of the marker – remove the marker). Cut the yarn, leaving a slightly longer tail than usual (for closing the armpit hole).

Set aside the 57 (61, 63) sleeve stitches and knit the other sleeve in the same way.

YOKE

Join the body and sleeves: Using 80 cm circular needles and MC, knit from the body to 5 (5, 6) sts before side marker. PM (this is the new round marker). Transfer the next 10 (10, 12) sts to waste yarn (remove side marker). K57 (61, 63) sts for one sleeve (this will be the left sleeve). Next, knit the body stitches until 5 (5, 6) sts remain before the original round marker. Transfer the next 10 (10, 12) sts to waste yarn (RM), k57 (61, 63) sts for the right sleeve, knit until new round marker. You should have 258 (282, 294) sts. The start of the round is now positioned at the seam between the back section and left sleeve. Knit 1 more round, decreasing 6 (2, 0) sts at even intervals. You should now have 252 (280, 294) sts. If you want a deeper yoke, you can continue in the MC for as long as you wish before beginning chart B.

Follow chart B: Work the rows of the chart, making decreases as indicated. The chart repeats 18 (20, 21) times per round. You should now have 90 (100, 105) sts.

Work the short rows: Begin by marking the mid-back with a stitch marker. Then knit to the marker and continue as follows:

Row 1 (RS): K10 (12, 14), turn work.

Row 2 (WS): Slip 1 st, p19 (23, 27), turn work.

Row 3: Slip 1 st, k29 (35, 41), turn work.

Row 4: Slip 1 st, p39 (47, 55), turn work.

Row 5: Slip 1 st, k49 (59, 69), turn work.

Row 6: Slip 1 st, p59 (71, 83), turn work and knit to round marker.

NECK

Knit 1 round in MC, decreasing 10 (16, 16) sts at even intervals. You should now have 80 (84, 89) sts.
Work in stocking stitch for 8 rounds.
Cast (bind) off using a stretchy cast-off method.
Allow the collar to roll up naturally.

FINISHING

Sew all the ends into the wrong side of the work.
Graft the armpit stitches. Wet the sweater and then squeeze dry. Shape and lay flat to dry.

"

Don't be afraid to try out Lapinvuokko with a darker main colour and white flowers – the white dryas is naturally white and bright throughout the summer, like snowflakes on the mountain heaths.

> Hallanvaara (Frosty Fell) is a classically beautiful sweater with a stranded pattern that repeats in the hem and the yoke. Hallanvaara is knitted from the hem up. The sleeves are knitted separately and joined to the body at the start of the yoke, and the neck is finished with I-cord.

Hallanvaara (Frosty Fell)

DESIGNER PIRJO IIVONEN

HALLANVAARA (FROSTY FELL)

MODEL SHOWN IS SIZE S

Sizes: S (M, L, XL)

Recommended positive ease 4–5 cm (1½–2 in).

Dimensions of finished sweater:

Chest circumference: 89 (94.5, 100, 105.5) cm (35 (37¼, 39⅜, 41½) in).

Length from armpit to hem: 45 (47, 49, 52) cm (17¾ (18½, 19¼, 20½) in).

Length from front collar to hem: 67 (71.5, 75.5, 79.5) cm (26⅜ (28⅛, 29¾, 31¼) in).

Circumference of upper sleeve: 34.5 (36.5, 39, 41) cm (13⅝ (14⅜, 15⅜, 16⅛) in).

Wrist circumference: 24.5 (24.5, 26.5, 26.5) cm (9⅝ (9⅝, 10½, 10½) in).

Inner sleeve length: 45 (48, 51, 53) cm (17¾ (18⅞, 20⅛, 20⅞) in).

Yarn (see conversions on page 11): Novita Icelandic Wool (100% wool; 90 m/50 g) or equivalent Aran/Worsted weight yarn.

MC: 044 Grafiitti 7 (9, 11, 13) balls or 630 (810, 990, 1170) m

CC1: 523 Puolukka 2 (2, 3, 3) balls or 180 (180, 270, 270) m

CC2: 045 Savi 4 (5, 6, 6) balls or 360 (450, 540, 540) m

Needles: Circular needles (40 and 80 cm/16 and 32 in) and double-pointed needles in sizes 4 mm (US 6) and 4.5 mm (US 7).

You will also need: Stitch markers, waste yarn or stitch holders, and a tapestry needle.

Tension (gauge): 18 sts and 23 rows = 10 × 10 cm (4 x 4 in) in stocking (stockinette) stitch, lightly blocked.

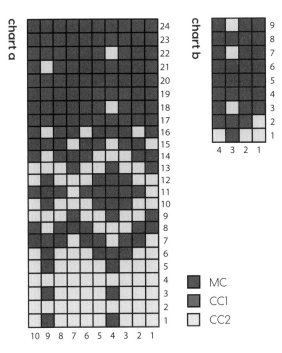

chart a

chart b

		9
		8
		7
		6
		5
		4
		3
		2
		1

4 3 2 1

■ MC
■ CC1
□ CC2

BODY

Using 4 mm needles and CC2, cast on 160 (170, 180, 190) sts. Join in the round, being careful not to twist the work. PM (this is positioned at the mid-back of the sweater).

Ribbing: *K1, p1, repeat from * to end.

Repeat this round until ribbing measures 5 cm (2 in). Switch to 4.5 mm needles. Work in stocking stitch for 1 round.

Follow chart A: Using MC and CCs 1 and 2, work the rows of the chart in stocking stitch. The pattern repeats 16 (17, 18, 19) times per round.

Once you've completed all 24 rows of the chart, cut CC1 and CC2.

Complete the body: Switch to 4 mm needles. Using MC, continue knitting in the round in stocking stitch the body measures 45 (47, 49, 52) cm (17¾ (18½, 19¼, 20½) in) from cast on edge. Set aside the body and knit the sleeves.

SLEEVES

Using 4 mm needles and CC2, cast on 44 (44, 48, 48) sts. Join in the round, being careful not to twist the work. PM (this is positioned at the inner sleeve).

Ribbing: *K1, p1, repeat from * to end.

Repeat this round until ribbing measures 5 cm (2 in). Switch to 4.5 mm needles and knit 1 round.

Follow chart B: Using MC and CCs 1 and 2, work the rows of the chart in stocking stitch. The pattern repeats 11 (11, 12, 12) times per round.

Once you have completed all 9 rows of the chart, cut CC1 and CC2.

Work the sleeve increases: Switch to 4 mm needles. Using MC, knit 1 round.

Increase round: K1, M1L, knit to last stitch, M1R, k1.
[2 sts increased – 46 (46, 48, 48) in total]
Repeat this increase round every 3 (3, 2.5, 2.5) cm (1¼ (1¼, 1, 1) in) a further 8 (10, 10, 12) times. You should now have 62 (66, 70, 74) sts.

Continue working in the round in stocking stitch
in MC until the sleeve measures 45 (48, 51, 53) cm
(17¾ (18¾, 20⅛, 20⅞) in) from cast-on edge.
Transfer 4 (5, 6, 7) sts from either side of the round
marker (a total of 8 (10, 12, 14) sts) onto waste yarn
for the armpit. 54 (56, 58, 60) sts now remain on
the needle for the sleeve.
Set aside and knit the other sleeve in the same way.

YOKE

Join the body and the sleeves: Using 4 mm needles
and MC, k36 (37, 39, 40) sts from the body for the
back left section, transfer the next 8 (10, 12, 14) sts
onto waste yarn to reserve for the left armpit, k54
(56, 58, 60) sleeve sts (this will be the left sleeve). K72
(76, 78, 82) sts from the body for the front section,
then transfer the next 8 (10, 12, 14) sts onto waste
yarn for the right armpit. Now k54 (56, 58, 60) sts to
join the right sleeve. Knit the remaining 36 (37, 39, 40)
sts from the body to complete the round. You should
now have 252 (262, 272, 282) sts.

Decrease round: Knit until there is 1 st of the left
sleeve remaining on the right needle, k2tog, knit until
there is 1 st of the right sleeve remaining on the right
needle, k2tog, knit to end of round. You should now
have 250 (260, 270, 280) sts.

Using MC, continue working in the round in stocking
stitch for a further 0 (3, 6, 8) rounds.

Follow chart C: Switch to 4.5 mm needles. Using MC
and CCs 1 and 2, work the rows of chart C, making
decreases as indicated. Please note:

Size S only: Leave out chart rows 25, 32, 42 and 50.

Size M only: Leave out chart rows 25 and 42.

The pattern repeats 25 (26, 27, 28) times per round.
At the start of row 24, switch to 4 mm needles,
cut MC and CC1 and continue with CC2 only. After
completing the chart, you should have 100 (104,
108, 112) sts and the yoke will be 21 (23, 25, 26) cm
(8¼ (9, 9⅞, 10¼) in) deep from the armpit.

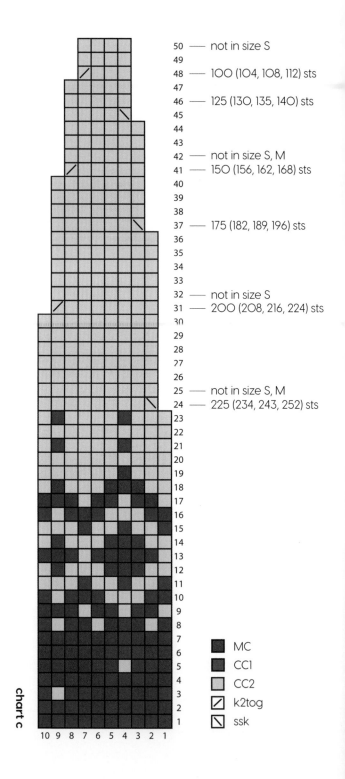

chart c

50 —— not in size S
49
48 —— 100 (104, 108, 112) sts
47
46 —— 125 (130, 135, 140) sts
45
44
43
42 —— not in size S, M
41 —— 150 (156, 162, 168) sts
40
39
38
37 —— 175 (182, 189, 196) sts
36
35
34
33
32 —— not in size S
31 —— 200 (208, 216, 224) sts
30
29
28
27
26
25 —— not in size S, M
24 —— 225 (234, 243, 252) sts
23
22
21
20
19
18
17
16
15
14
13
12
11
10
9
8
7
6
5
4
3
2
1

10 9 8 7 6 5 4 3 2 1

- ■ MC
- ■ CC1
- □ CC2
- ◪ k2tog
- ◩ ssk

NECK

Work the short rows for the neck: Knit a small elevation in the back using short rows as follows:

Row 1 (RS): K10 (10, 10, 10) sts, turn work.

Row 2 (WS): Make a DS, purl to round marker, SM, p10 (10, 10, 10), turn work.

Row 3: Make a DS, knit to round marker, SM, knit to DS, knit the DS as a single stitch, k7 (7, 7, 7), turn work.

Row 4: Make a DS, purl to round marker, SM, purl to DS, purl the DS as a single stitch, p7 (7, 7, 7), turn work.

Row 5: Make a DS, knit to round marker, SM, knit to DS, knit the DS as a single stitch, k7 (7, 7, 7), turn work.

Row 6: Make a DS, purl to round marker, SM, purl to DS, purl the DS as a single stitch, p7 (7, 7, 7), turn work.

Row 7: Make a DS, knit to round marker, SM, knit to end of round, knitting each DS as a single stitch.

Decrease round:

Size S only: K2, (k2tog, k3) 19 times, k2tog, k1 [20 sts decreased – 80 sts remaining]

Size M only: K2, (k2og, k4) 2 times, (k2tog, k3) 15 times, (k2tog, k4) 2 times, k2tog, k1. [20 sts decreased – 84 sts remaining]

Size L only: K2, (k2tog, k2) 6 times, (k2tog, k3) 11 times, (k2tog, k2) 6 times, k2tog, k1. [24 sts decreased – 84 sts remaining]

Size XL only: K2, (k2tog, k2) 4 times, (k2tog, k3) 15 times, (k2tog, k2) 4 times, k2tog, k1. [24 sts decreased – 88 sts remaining]

Next round (all sizes): Knit to end.

Finish with I-cord: Use the I-cord cast-off (bind-off) method to finish the neck. Cast on 4 new stitches as follows: insert the right needle into the first stitch on the left needle knitwise, pass the yarn over the needle from behind and pull a loop of it through to the front on the right needle as if to knit but, at this point, instead of pulling the starting stitch off the left needle, leave it there and. Instead, rotate the left needle forwards and pass into the new loop from below to transfer the loop onto the left needle, creating a new stitch. Cast on 3 more stitches in this way to give you 4 I-cord stitches at the start of the round.

Cast-off round: *K3, k2tog tbl (you're knitting together the final I-cord st and the first of your original sts on the needle). Now transfer the 4 sts on the right needle to the left needle, keeping the yarn at the back of the work. Pull tight on the yarn, then repeat from * to final 4 sts. Cast off 4 sts. Cut the yarn and sew the start and end stitches together.

FINISHING

Graft the armpits and sew the ends into the wrong side of the work. Wash the sweater in lukewarm water, squeeze inside a towel to remove excess water, shape it on a flat surface, and leave to dry.

"

Deep among the trees,
bathed in moonlight,
a fox prowls the forest.

"

It's up to you where you wish to place the fox on the yoke of this sweater. The pattern instructions will help you to position it wherever you decide. The front and back section are identical but, if you wish, you can shape the back of the neck using short rows. Because the sweater is knitted from the top down, you can lengthen it by frogging the ribbing, then knitting more length into the sleeves and front. This way, your little one won't grow out of it too soon.

Kettumetsä (Foxes Forest)

DESIGNER MINTTU WIKBERG

KETTUMETSÄ (FOXES FOREST) / CHILDREN

MODEL SHOWN IS SIZE 100 CM (39⅜ IN)

Sizes (height): 100 (120, 140, 160) cm
(39⅜, (47¼, 55⅛, 63) in).
Recommended positive ease approx. 12 cm (4¾ in).

Dimensions of finished sweater:

Chest circumference: 69 (75.5, 84.5, 93.5) cm
(27⅛ (29¾, 33¼, 36¾) in).

Length from armpit to hem:
24.5 (28.5, 32.5, 37.5) cm (9⅝ (11¼, 12¾, 14¾) in).

Length from front collar to hem:
39.5 (44.5, 50.5, 56.5) cm (15½ (17½, 19⅞, 22¼) in).

Circumference of upper sleeve: 26.5 (28, 32, 34.5) cm
(10½ (11, 12⅝, 13⅝) in).

Wrist circumference: 18 (18, 20, 22) cm (7 (7, 7⅞, 8⅝) in.

Inner sleeve length: 29.5 (34.5, 41.5, 50.5) cm
(11⅝ (13⅝, 16⅜, 19⅞) in).

Yarn (see conversions on page 11): Novita Icelandic
Wool (100% wool; 90 m/50 g) or equivalent Aran/
Worsted weight yarn.

MC: 045 Savi 4 (6, 7, 8) balls or 380 (540, 630, 720) m

CC1: 010 Luonnonvalkoinen 1 (1, 1, 1) balls or
15 (20, 30, 40) m

CC2: 164 Mustikka 1 (1, 1, 1) ball or 20 (30, 40, 50) m

CC3: 663 Tatti 1 (1, 1, 1) ball or 40 (50, 70, 80) m

CC4: 638 Seitikki 1 (1, 1, 2) ball(s) or 50 (70, 90, 100) m

Needles: Circular needles (40 and 80 cm/16 and
32 in) and double-pointed needles in sizes 4 mm (US 6)
and 4.5 mm (US 7).

You will also need: Stitch markers, waste yarn or
stitch holders, and a tapestry needle.

Tension (gauge): 18 sts and 25 rows = 10 × 10 cm
(4 x 4 in) in stocking (stockinette) stitch, lightly blocked.

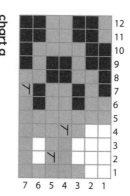

chart a

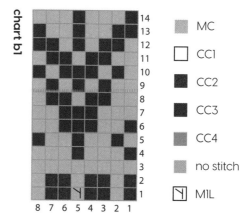

chart b1

	MC
	CC1
	CC2
	CC3
	CC4
	no stitch
	M1L

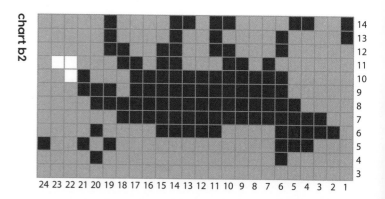

chart b2

YOKE

Using 4 mm needles and CC4, cast on 78 (84, 86, 90) sts. Join in the round, ensuring not to twist the row of sts. PM. Join MC.

Ribbing: *K1 in CC4, p1 in MC, repeat from * to end. Repeat this round until ribbing measures 2.5 (2.5, 3, 3) cm (1 (1, 1¼, 1¼) in).

Increase round: Switch to 4.5 mm needles. Using MC and working in stocking stitch, work an increase round as follows:

Size 100 only: K1, *k5, M1L, k6, M1L, repeat from *to end. *[14 sts increased – 92 sts in total]*

Size 120 only: *(K5, M1L) 3 times, k6, M1L, repeat from * to end. *[16 sts increased – 100 sts in total]*

Size 140 only: K1, M1L, *k3, M1L, k4, M1L, repeat from * until 1 st remains, k1, M1L. *[26 sts increased – 112 sts in total]*

Size 160 only: K5, M1L, *k3, M1L, k2, M1L, repeat from * until 5 sts remain, k5, M1L. *[34 sts increased – 124 sts in total]*

(All sizes) If you are *not* working short rows for the neck

Using MC, continue working in stocking stitch for a further 1 (2, 3, 4) rounds.

(All sizes) If you *are* working short rows for the neck: For a raised neck, work the following short rows. Each time you reach a DS made previously, remember to knit it as a single stitch.

Row 1 (RS): K27 (30, 33, 37) sts, turn work.

Row 2 (WS): Make a DS, purl to the round marker, turn work.

Row 3 (RS): Make a DS, k42 (46, 50, 55) sts (knit the DS as a single stitch), turn work.

Row 4 (WS): Make a DS, p57 (62, 67, 73) sts. Turn the work.

Row 5 (RS): Make a DS and knit to the round marker (knitting each DS as a single stitch).

Follow chart A: Using MC and CCs 1 and 2, work the rows of the chart in stocking stitch, making increases as indicated. The chart repeats 23 (25, 28, 31) times per round. When you have completed all 12 rows of the chart, you should have 161, (175, 196, 217) sts.

Follow charts B1 and B2: Using MC and CCs 1, 2, and 3, work the rows of charts B1 and B2 as follows.

Round 1: Knit row 1 of chart B1, making increases as indicated. The chart repeats 23 (25, 28, 31) times per round. You should now have 184 (200, 224, 248) sts.

Round 2: Knit row 2 of chart B1.

Rounds 3–14: You will be working mainly with chart B1 for these rounds, but use chart B2 to replace 3 of the pattern repeats from chart B1 to create the fox pattern. You can position the fox wherever on the yoke you would like it to appear. (The first 54 (60, 66, 74) sts will form the back, the next 38 (40, 46, 50) sts will form the top of the left sleeve, the next 54 (60, 66, 74) sts will form the front, and the last 38 (40, 46, 50) sts will form the top of the right sleeve.) The fox's eye is embroidered to trace the stitches, so is worked in MC at this point. When you have completed all rows of charts B1 and B2, cut the CCs.

Complete the yoke: Using MC and working in stocking stitch, continue to work in the round until the yoke measures at least 15 (16, 18, 19) cm (6 (6¼, 7, 7½) in) from cast-on edge.

Separate the body and sleeves: K54 (60, 66, 74) sts for the back, transfer the next 38 (40, 46, 50) sts for the right sleeve onto waste yarn, then cast on 8 (8, 10, 10) sts for the right armpit directly after the stitches you just knitted for the back. K54 (60, 66, 74) sts for the front, transfer the next 38 (40, 46, 50) sts to waste yarn for the left sleeve, and cast on 8 (8, 10, 10) sts for the left armpit directly after the stitches you just knitted for the front. The body now has 124 (136, 152, 168) sts.

BODY

Using MC and working in stocking stitch, continue working in the round until the work measures 20 (24, 28, 33) cm. (7⅞ (9½, 11, 13) in) from the armpit.

Ribbing: Switch to 4 mm needles. *K1 in CC4, p1 in MC, repeat from * to end.

Repeat this round until ribbing measures 4.5 cm (1¾ in). Cut MC.

Next round: Using CC4, *k1, p1, repeat from * to end. Cast (bind) off using CC4.

SLEEVES

Transfer the 38 (40, 46, 50) sts for one sleeve from waste yarn onto 4.5 mm circular needles. Pick up 8 (8, 10, 10) sts from the armpit stitches you previously cast on, and pick up 1 st from each side of the divide between the armpit stitches and yoke to prevent holes. You should now have 48 (50, 58, 62) sts. Join in the round. PM at the centre armpit, at the halfway point of the newly picked up sts.

Continue working in the round in stocking stitch until the sleeve measures 3 (1, 1, 3) cm (1¼ (⅜, ⅜, 1¼) in) from armpit.

Work the sleeve decreases: Decreases are worked at the ends and beginnings of rounds, on either side of the round marker.

Decrease round 1: Knit to last 2 sts, k2tog tbl.

Decrease round 2: K2tog, k to end. *[2 sts decreased – 46 (48, 56, 60 in total]*

Repeat these 2 decrease rounds once every 3 (3.5, 3.5, 4) cm (1¼ (1⅜, 1⅜, 1½) in) a further 7 (8, 10, 10) times. You should now have 32 (32, 36, 40) sts.

Complete the sleeve: Continue working in the round in stocking stitch until the sleeve measures 26 (30, 37, 46) cm (10¼, (11¾, 14½, 18⅛) in) from armpit.

Ribbing: Switch to 4 mm needles. Using MC and CC4, *k1 in CC4, p1 in MC, repeat from * to end. Repeat this round until ribbing measures 3.5 (4.5, 4.5, 4.5) cm (1⅜ (1¾, 1¾, 1¾) in). Cut MC.

Next round: Using CC4.,*k1, p1, repeat from * to end. Cast (bind) off using CC4.

FINISHING

Sew in the ends on the wrong side of the work. Embroider the eye onto the fox, tracing the stitches. Carefully dampen the work (try using a spray bottle). Shape the sweater, then lay flat to dry.

KETTUMETSÄ (FOXES FOREST)

Sizes: S (M, L, XL)
Recommended positive ease 12 cm (4¾ in).

Dimensions of finished sweater:
Chest circumference: 101 (110, 116.5, 123.5) cm (39¾ (43¼, 45⅞, 48⅝) in).
Length from armpit to hem:
38.5 (39.5, 40.5, 41.5) cm (15⅛ (15½, 16, 16⅜) in).
Length from front collar to hem:
59.5 (62.5, 65.5, 67.5) cm (23⅜ (24⅝, 25¾, 26⅝) in).
Circumference of upper sleeve: 36.5 (40, 42, 44.5) cm (14⅜ (15¾, 16½, 17½) in).
Wrist circumference: 23.5 (24.5, 25.5, 26.5) cm (9¼ (9⅝, 10, 10½) in).
Inner sleeve length: 47.5 (49.5, 50.5, 50.5) cm (18¾ (19½, 19⅞, 19⅞) in.

Yarn (see conversions on page 11): Novita Icelandic Wool (100% wool; 90 m/50 g) or equivalent Aran/Worsted weight yarn.
MC: 045 Savi 8 (9, 10, 11) balls or 720 (810, 900, 990) m
CC1: 010 Luonnonvalkoinen 1 (1, 1, 1) ball or 50 (60, 70, 90) m
CC2: 164 Mustikka 1 (1, 1, 2) ball(s) or 60 (70, 90, 110) m
CC3: 663 Tatti 2 (2, 2, 2) balls or 120 (140, 160, 180) m
CC4: 638 Seitikki 2 (2, 3, 3) balls or 160 (180, 210, 250) m

Needles: Circular needles (40 and 80 cm/16 and 32 in) and double-pointed needles in sizes 4 mm (US 6) and 4.5 mm (US 7)

You will also need: Stitch markers, waste yarn or stitch holders, and a tapestry needle.

Tension (gauge): 18 sts and 25 rows = 10 × 10 cm (4 x 4 in) in stocking (stockinette) stitch, lightly blocked.

YOKE

Using 4 mm needles and CC4, cast on 96 (100, 108, 116) sts. Join in the round, ensuring not to twist the row of stitches. PM. Join MC.

Ribbing: *K1 in CC4, p1 in MC, repeat from * to end. Repeat this round until ribbing measures 3 cm (1¼ in).

Increase round: Switch to 4.5 mm needles. Using MC and working in stocking stitch, work an increase round as follows:

Size S only: *K8, M1L, repeat from *to end. *[12 sts increased – 108 sts in total]*

Size M only: K4, *k6, M1L, repeat from * to end. *[16 sts increased – 116 sts in total]*

Size L only: K2, *k6, M1L, k7, M1L, repeat from * to last 2 sts, k2. *[16 sts increased – 124 sts in total]*

Size XL only: K2, *k7, M1L, repeat from *to last 2 sts, k2. *[16 sts increased – 132 sts in total]*

(All sizes) If you are *not* working short rows (to create a symmetrical neckline at front and back): Using MC, continue in stocking stitch for a further 3 (4, 5, 6) rounds.

(All sizes) If you *are* working short rows: For a raised neck, work the following short rows. Each time you reach a DS you have made previously, remember to knit it as a single stitch.

Row 1 (RS): K33 (35, 38, 40) sts, turn work,

Row 2 (WS): Make a DS, purl to round marker. Turn work.

Row 3 (RS): Make a DS, k50 (54, 58, 62) sts, turn work.

Row 4 (WS): Make a DS, p67 (73, 78, 84) sts. Turn work.

Row 5 (RS): Make a DS, knit to the round marker.

Follow chart A: Using MC and CCs 1 and 2, work the rows of the chart in stocking stitch, making increases as indicated. (In row 1, when you reach each DS, ensure you knit it together as 1 st.) The charted pattern repeats 27 (29, 31, 33) times per round. When you have completed all 12 rows of the chart, you should have 189, (203, 217, 231) sts.

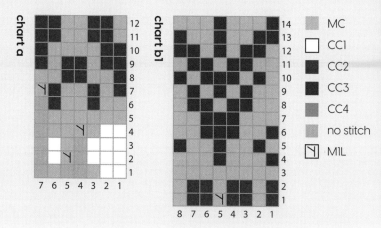

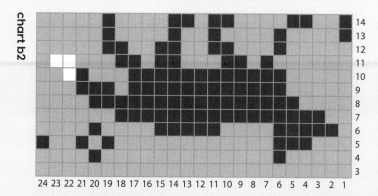

Follow charts B1 and B2: Using MC and CCs 1, 2, and 3, work the rows of charts B1 and B2 as follows.

Round 1: Knit row 1 of chart B1, making increases as indicated. The chart repeats 27 (29, 32, 33) times per round. You should now have 216 (232, 248, 264) sts.

Round 2: Knit row 2 of chart B1.

Rounds 3–14: You will be working mainly with chart B1 for these rounds, but use chart B2 to replace 3 of the pattern repeats from chart B1 to create the fox pattern. You can position the fox wherever on the yoke you would like it to appear. (The first 66 (70, 76, 80) sts will form the back, the next 42 (46, 48, 52) sts will form the left sleeve, the next 66 (70, 76, 80) sts will form the front, and the last 42 (46, 48, 52) sts will form the left sleeve. The fox's eye is embroidered to trace the stitches, so is worked in MC at this point. When you have completed all rows of charts B1 and B2, cut CCs 1 and 3.

Using MC, knit 1 round in stocking stitch.

Increase round 1: *K8, M1L, repeat from * to end. *[27 (29, 31, 33) sts increased – 243 (261, 279, 297) sts total]* Knit 1 round in stocking stitch.

Increase round 2: *K9, M1L, repeat from * to end. *[27 (29, 31, 33) sts increased – 270 (290, 310, 330) sts in total]*

Follow chart C: Using MC and CC2, work the rows of chart C in stocking stitch. The pattern repeats 27 (29, 31, 33) times per round. When you have competed all 3 rows of chart C, cut CC2.

Complete the yoke: Using MC, continue to work in the round in stocking stitch until the yoke measures at least 21 (23, 25, 26) cm (8¼ (9, 9⅞, 10¼) in) from cast-on edge.

Separate the body and sleeves: K81 (87, 93, 99) sts for the back section, transfer the next 54 (58, 62, 66) sts to waste yarn to reserve for the right sleeve, cast on 10 (12, 12, 12) sts directly after the stitches you just knitted for the sweater's back, for the right armpit, k81 (87, 93, 99) sts for the front section, transfer the next 54 (58, 62, 66) sts to waste yarn to reserve for the left sleeve, cast on 10 (12 12, 12) sts for the left armpit. The body now has 182 (198, 210, 222) sts.

BODY

Using MC, continue working in the round in stocking stitch until the work measures 33 (34, 35, 36) cm. (13 (13½, 14, 14⅛) in).

Ribbing: Switch to 4 mm needles. Using MC and CC4, *k1 in CC4, p1 in MC, repeat from * to end. Repeat this round until ribbing measures 5.5 cm (2¼ in). Cut MC.

Next round: Using CC4, *k1, p1, repeat from * to end. Cast (bind) off using CC4.

SLEEVES

Transfer the 54 (58, 62, 66) sts for one sleeve from waste yarn onto 4.5 mm needles. Using MC, pick up 10 (12 12, 12) sts from the armpit sts you previously cast on, and pick up 1 st from each side of the divide between the armpit stitches and yoke to prevent holes. You should now have 66 (72, 76, 80) sts. Join in the round. PM at the centre armpit, at the mid point of the newly picked up sts.

Continue working in the round in stocking stitch until the work measures 2 cm (¾ in) from the armpit.

Work the sleeve decreases: Decreases are worked at the ends and beginnings of rounds, on either side of the round marker.

Decrease round 1: Knit to last 2 sts, k2tog tbl.

Decrease round 2: K2tog, k to end. *[2 sts decreased – 64 (70, 74, 78) sts in total]*

Repeat these 2 decrease rounds once every 4 (3.5, 3.5, 3.5) cm (1½ (1⅜, 1⅜, 1⅜) in) a further 11 (13, 14, 15) times. You should now have 42 (44, 46, 48) sts.

Complete the sleeve: Continue working in the round in stocking stitch until the sleeve measures 42 (44, 45, 45) cm (16½ (17⅜, 17¾, 17¾) in).

Ribbing: Switch to 4 mm needles. Using MC and CC4, *k1 in CC4, p1 in MC, repeat from * to end. Repeat the last round until ribbing measures 5.5 cm (2¼ in). Cut MC.

Next round: Using CC4, *k1, p1, repeat from * to end. Cast off using CC4.

FINISHING

Follow the finishing instructions given on page 110.

"

Terra gets its name and colour scheme from the snow thawing in the spring, revealing the earth and all its wonderful scents. I always miss the smell of thawed earth during the long winter! The sweater's yoke also features glimpses of the bright turquoise sky, with the sun peeking out and bringing with it the promise of spring and summer. This sweater is knitted from the hem up.

Terra

DESIGNER ANNIKA KONTTANIEMI

TERRA

Sizes: S (M, L, XL)

Recommended positive ease 5–10 cm (2–4 in).

Dimensions of finished sweater:

Chest circumference: 106.5 (117.5, 128, 138.5) cm (41⅞ (46¼, 50⅜, 54½) in).

Length from armpit to hem: 42 (43, 44, 45) cm (16½ (17, 17⅜, 17¾) in).

Length from front collar to hem: 66 (67, 69, 70.5) cm (26 (26⅜, 27⅛, 27¾) in).

Circumference of upper sleeve: 40 (41.5, 42.5, 45.5) cm (15¾ (16⅜, 16¾, 17⅞) in).

Wrist circumference: 26.5 (26.5, 32, 32) cm (10½ (10½, 12⅝, 12⅝) in).

Inner sleeve length: 46 cm (18⅛ in).

Yarn (see conversions on page 11): Ístex Léttlopi (100% wool; 100 m/50 g) or equivalent Aran/Worsted weight yarn.

MC: 9426 Golden Heather 6 (7, 7, 9) balls or 600 (700, 700, 900) m

CC1: 1418 Straw 2 (2, 2, 2) balls or 200 (200, 200, 200) m

CC2: 1414 Violet Heather 1 (1, 1, 1) ball or 100 (100, 100, 100) m

CC3: 9423 Lagoon Heather 1 (1, 1, 1) ball or 100 (100, 100, 100) m

CC4: 1404 Glacier Blue Heather 1 (1, 1, 1) ball or 100 (100, 100, 100) m

Needles: Circular needles (80 and 100 cm/32 and 40 in) and double-pointed needles in sizes 3.5 mm (US 4) and 4.5 mm (US 7).

You will also need: Stitch markers, waste yarn or stitch holders, and a tapestry needle.

Tension (gauge): 15 sts and 21 rows = 10 × 10 cm (4 x 4 in) in stocking (stockinette) stitch, lightly blocked.

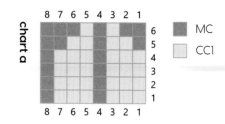

chart a

MC

CC1

BODY

Using 3.5 mm needles and CC1, cast on 160 (176, 192, 208) sts. Do not join in the round – work the first row flat.

Initial row: *K1, p1, repeat from * to end.

Join in the round, ensuring not to twist the row of stitches. PM (this is positioned at the right side).

Ribbing: *K1, p1, repeat from * to end.

Repeat this round until ribbing measures 6 cm (2⅜ in).

Next round: Switch to 4.5 mm needles. Knit to end.

Follow chart A: Using MC and CC1, work the rows of the chart in stocking stitch. The pattern repeats 20 (22, 24, 26) times per round. Once you have completed all 6 rows of the chart, cut CC1.

Work the short rows to lengthen the back hem:

Row 1 (RS): Using MC, k102 (112, 122, 132) sts, w&t.

Row 2 (WS): Purl to round marker, SM, p22 (24, 26, 28), w&t.

Row 3: Knit to round marker, SM, k94 (104, 114, 124), w&t.

Row 4: Purl to round marker, SM, p14 (16, 18, 20), w&t.

Row 5: Knit to round marker, SM, k86 (96, 106, 116), w&t.

Row 6: Purl to round marker, SM, p6 (8, 10, 12), w&t.

Row 7: Knit to round marker, SM, k80 (88, 96, 104), w&t.

Row 8: Purl to round marker, SM, w&t.

Next round: Knit to end, picking up the wraps and knitting them together with the stitches.

Using MC, continue working in the round in stocking stitch until the body measures 42 (43, 44, 45) cm (16½, (17, 17⅜, 17¾) in) from centre front.

Separate the body and sleeves: RM, transfer the next 5 (5, 6, 7) sts to waste yarn for the right armpit, k70 (77, 84, 90) sts for the back section, transfer the next 10 (11, 12, 14) sts to another piece of waste yarn for the left armpit, k70 (77, 84, 90) sts for the front section, transfer the final 5 (6, 6, 7) sts onto the first piece of waste yarn to complete the sts reserved for the right armpit. Set aside while you knit the sleeves.

SLEEVES

Using 3.5 mm needles and CC1, cast on 40 (40, 44, 48) sts. Do not join in the round – work the first row flat.

Initial row: *K1, p1, repeat from * to end.

Join in the round, ensuring not to twist the row of stitches. PM (this is placed at the inner sleeve).

Next round: *K1, p1, repeat from * to end.

Repeat this round until ribbing measures 6 cm (2⅜ in)

Next round: Switch to 4.5 mm needles. Knit 1 round in CC1, increasing 0 (0, 4, 0) sts at even intervals. You should now have 40 (40, 48, 48) sts.

Follow chart A: Using MC and CC1, work the rows of the chart in stocking stitch. The pattern repeats 5 (5, 6, 6) times per round. Once you have completed all 6 rows of the chart, cut CC1.

Work the sleeve increases: Using MC, continue to work in the round in stocking stitch for 4 more rounds.

Increase round: K1, M1, knit to last stitch, M1, k1.
[2 sts increased]

Repeat this increase round once every 7th (6th, 9th, 7th) round a further 9 (10, 7, 9) times. You should now have 60 (62, 64, 68) sts.

Using MC, continue working in the round in stocking stitch until the sleeve measures 46 cm (18⅛ in).

Next round: Transfer the first 5 (5, 6, 7) sts to waste yarn, knit until 5 (6, 6, 7) sts remain, transfer these remaining sts to the same waste yarn. You now have 50 (51, 52, 54) sts for the sleeve.

Set aside and knit the other sleeve in the same way.

YOKE

Join the body and sleeves: Using 4.5 mm needles and MC, k70 (77, 84, 90) from the body for the back section, join the first (left) sleeve by knitting the 50 (51, 52, 54) sts, knit the remaining 70 (77, 84, 90) sts from the body for the front section, then join the second (right) sleeve by knitting the 50 (51, 52, 54) sts. PM (this is now positioned at the join between the right sleeve and the back section). (If you wish, you can use the 3-needle cast (bind) off technique to seam together the armpit sts during this joining round.) You should now have 240 (256, 272, 288) sts.

Follow chart B: Using MC and CCs 1, 2, 3, and 4, work the rows of the chart, making decreases as indicated. The pattern repeats 30 (32, 34, 36) times per round. When you have completed all 49 rows of the chart, cut the CCs. You should now have 60 (64, 68, 72) sts.

Complete the yoke: Using MC, continue working in the round in stocking stitch for a further 0 (0, 2, 4) rounds. The depth of the yoke from the armpit is now 24 (24, 25, 25.5) cm (9½ (9½, 9⅞, 10) in.

NECK

Knit a small elevation at the back using short rows.

Row 1 (RS): K38 (40, 42, 45), w&t.

Row 2 (WS): Purl to round marker, SM, p8 (8, 8, 9), w&t.

Row 3: Knit to round marker, SM, k32 (34, 36, 38), w&t.

Row 4: Purl to round marker, SM, p2 (2, 2, 2), w&t.

Row 5: Knit to round marker.

Using MC, continue working in the round in stocking stitch for a further 5 rounds. Cast off loosely.

FINISHING

Cast off the armpit stitches by grafting them or using the 3-needle cast off. Sew in the ends and finish the sweater by wetting or steaming it.

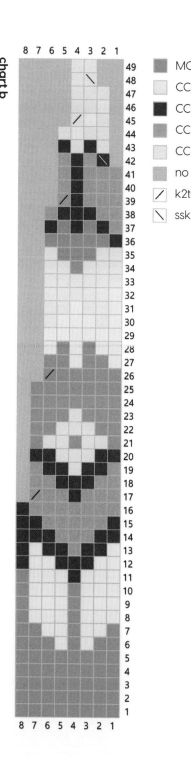

chart b

	MC
	CC1
	CC2
	CC3
	CC4
	no stitch
/	k2tog
\	ssk

"

The short rows knitted at the back hem and in the neck give this sweater extra length at the rear, to help keep your lower back warm and cosy.

Ethän revi
tu...hta
elä...stä
puista!

...LITUS

"

What a wonderful way to showcase the colourful variation in natural Finnsheep wool! The lanolin that naturally occurs in the yarn makes for an extremely weatherproof sweater for kids who like to spend time outdoors. If the sweater becomes dirty in something wet, like slush, first let it dry out, then scratch off the worst of the dirt. Knitted from the hem up, this sweater is made using the stranded knitting technique throughout, and is consequently very warm – almost like a jacket.

Lampurin läppi (Little Shepherd)

DESIGNER ANNIKA KONTTANIEMI

LAMPURIN LÄPPI (LITTLE SHEPHERD)

MODEL SHOWN IS SIZE 110 CM (43¼ IN)

Sizes: 90 (110, 130, 150) cm (43¼ (51¼, 59) in).
Recommended positive ease 5–10 cm (2–4 in).

Dimensions of finished sweater:
Chest circumference: 60 (70, 80, 90) cm (23⅝ (27½, 31½, 35½) in).
Length from armpit to hem: 32.5 cm (12¾ in).
Length from front collar to hem:
49.5 (49.5, 53, 53) cm (19½ (19½, 20⅞, 20⅞) in).
Circumference of upper sleeve:
20 (24, 27.5, 30) cm (7⅞ (9½, 10⅞, 11¾) in).
Wrist circumference: 15 (20, 20, 20) cm (6 (7⅞, 7⅞, 7⅞) in).
Inner sleeve length: 29 (29, 32.5, 32.5) cm (11½ (11½, 12¾, 12¾) in).

Yarn (see conversions on page 11): Vanhalan lammastila's 3-ply carded yarn (100% Finnsheep wool; 230 m/100 g) or equivalent DK/Light Worsted weight yarn.
MC: Light Brown 1 (1, 1, 1) skein or 230 (230, 230, 230) m
CC1: Medium Brown 1 (1, 1, 1) skein or 230 (230, 230, 230) m
CC2: Natural White 1 (1, 1, 1) skein or 230 (230, 230, 230) m
CC3: Light Grey 1 (1, 1, 1) skein or 230 (230, 230, 230) m
CC4: Black 1 (1, 1, 1) skein or 230 (230, 230, 230) m
CC5: Dark Grey 1 (1, 1, 1) skein or 230 (230, 230, 230) m

Needles: Circular needles (80 and 100 cm)/32 and 40 in) and double-pointed needles in sizes 4.5 mm (US 7) and 5 mm (US 8).

You will also need: Stitch marker, waste yarn or stitch holders, tapestry needle.

Tension (gauge): 16 sts and 19 rows = 10 × 10 cm (4 × 4 in) in stranded stocking (stockinette) stitch, lightly blocked.

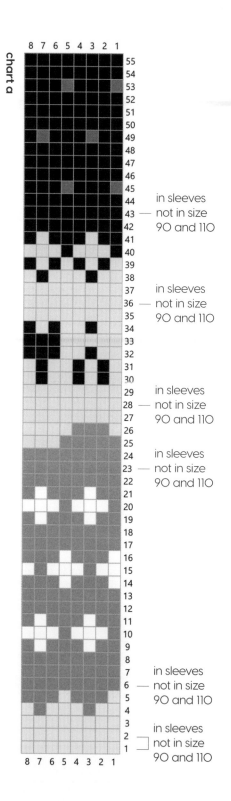

chart a

in sleeves — not in size 90 and 110 (43, 42)

in sleeves — not in size 90 and 110 (37, 36, 35)

in sleeves — not in size 90 and 110 (29, 28, 27)

in sleeves — not in size 90 and 110 (24, 23, 22)

in sleeves — not in size 90 and 110 (7, 6, 5)

in sleeves — not in size 90 and 110 (3, 2, 1)

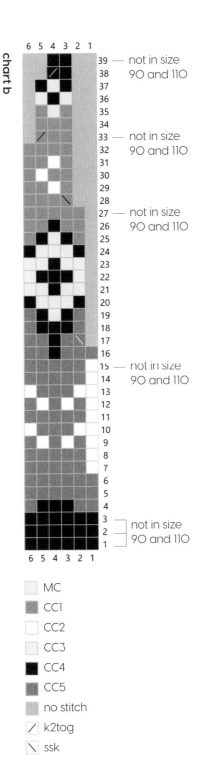

left side of chart

chart b

6 5 4 3 2 1

39 — not in size
38   90 and 110
37
36
35
34
33 — not in size
32   90 and 110
31
30
29
28
27 — not in size
26   90 and 110
25
24
23
22
21
20
19
18
17
16
15 — not in size
14   90 and 110
13
12
11
10
9
8
7
6
5
4
3 ⎤ not in size
2 ⎬ 90 and 110
1 ⎦

6 5 4 3 2 1

☐ MC
▨ CC1
☐ CC2
▨ CC3
■ CC4
▨ CC5
▨ no stitch
◸ k2tog
◺ ssk

BODY

Using 4.5 mm needles and MC, cast on 96 (112, 128, 144) sts. Join in the round, Join in the round, ensuring not to twist the row of stitches. PM.

Ribbing: K1, p1, repeat from * to end.
Repeat this round 6 more times.

Follow chart A: Switch to 5 mm needles. Using MC and CCs 1, 2, 3, 4, and 5, work rows 1–54 of the chart in stocking stitch. The pattern repeats 12 (14, 16, 18) times per round.

Row 55: Transfer the last 2 (2, 3, 3) sts of the previous round to waste yarn, RM, k2 (3, 3, 3) sts according to the chart, then transfer them to the same waste yarn. Following the chart, k48 (56, 64, 72) sts, then transfer the last 4 (5, 6, 6) sts you have just knitted to waste yarn. Knit to end of round following the chart. You now have 88 (102, 116, 132) sts for the body (44 (51, 58, 66) sts for each of the front and back sections).

Set aside the body and knit the sleeves.

SLEEVES

Using 4.5 mm needles and MC, cast on 24 (32, 32, 32) sts. Join in the round, ensuring not to twist the row of stitches. PM.

Ribbing: *K1, p1, repeat from * to end.
Repeat this round 6 more times.

Follow chart A/sleeve increases: Switch to 5 mm needles. Using MC and CCs 1, 2, 3, 4, and 5, work the rows of the chart. The pattern repeats 3 (4, 4, 4) times per round.

Sizes 90 and 110 only: Skip chart rows 1, 2, 6, 23, 28, 36 and 43.

(All sizes) *At the same time,* work the sleeve increases. Increase rounds are as follows:

K1, M1L, follow the chart until 1 st remains, M1R, k1. Work the first increase round when working the first chart row, then repeat it once every 12th (16th, 9th, 6th) round a further 3 (2, 5, 7) times. The work now

has 32 (38, 44, 48) sleeve stitches. Note that the sleeve pattern will not distribute evenly due to the increases. At the beginning of an increase round, ensure you account for the increase and begin working the charted pattern at the same point on the sleeve circumference. Work the increased sts in MC. When you have completed all 55 rows of the chart, cut the yarns. Transfer the last 2 (2, 3, 3) sts of the round to waste yarn, RM, then transfer the first 2 (3, 3, 3) sts to the same waste yarn . *[28 (33, 38, 42) sleeve stitches]* Knit the other sleeve in the same way.

YOKE

Join body and sleeves/follow chart B: Using 5 mm needles and CCs 1, 2, 3, 4, work the rows of chart B in stocking stitch, joining the body and sleeves during the first round of the chart as follows: k44 (51, 58, 66) sts from the body for the back section, join the first (left) sleeve by knitting the 28 (33, 38, 42) sts, knit the last 44, (51, 58, 66) body sts for the front section, join the second (right) sleeve by knitting the 28 (33, 38, 42) sts. PM. (If you wish, use the 3-needle cast (bind) off method during this round to cast off the armpit stitches from both sleeve and body together to close the gap.) You now have 144 (168, 192, 216) sts. Note: **Sizes 90 and 110 only:** Skip chart rows 1–3, 15, 27, 33 and 39. This means you begin the chart/join the body and sleeves on row 4.
Once you have completed chart B, you should have 48 (56, 64, 72) sts.
Complete the neck: Switch to 4.5 mm needles. Using CC4, work in stocking stitch for 10 rounds. Cast off loosely.

FINISHING

Sew in all the ends. Finish the sweater by dampening or steaming it lightly.

> This sweater is great for using up little bits of leftover yarn – you can use as many colours as you have around! As there is stranded knitting throughout, ensure your tension (gauge) is the same as stated in the pattern to avoid knitting the sweater too small. If you like, you can make it easier to knit by using just one colour.

"

Rakovalkealla is a gorgeous and warm sweater made from Álafosslopi yarn. It is quick to knit up on thick needles, and there is only one row of stranded knitting in which you knit with all three colours, so as Fair Isle knitting goes, this one is comparatively easy!

Rakovalkealla (Around the log fire)

DESIGNER MERJA OJANPERÄ

RAKOVALKEALLA (AROUND THE LOG FIRE)

MODEL SHOWN IS SIZE M

Sizes: S (M, L)

Recommended positive ease approx. 5 cm (2 in).

Dimensions of finished sweater:
Chest circumference: 90 (98.5, 111.5) cm (35½ (38¾, 43⅞) in).
Length from armpit to hem: 47 cm (18½ in).
Length from front collar to hem: 69 (71.5, 73) cm (27⅛ (28⅛, 28¾) in).
Circumference of upper sleeve: 38.5 (43, 51.5) cm (15⅛ (17, 20¼) in).
Wrist circumference: 28.5 (28.5, 31.5) cm (11¼ (11¼, 12⅜) in).
Inner sleeve length: 46 (48, 50) cm (18⅛ (18⅞, 19⅝) in).

Yarn (see conversions on page 11): Ístex Álafosslopi (100% Icelandic wool; 100 m/100 g) or equivalent Chunky/Bulky weight yarn.
MC: 0051 White 5 (5, 6) balls or 500 (500, 600) m
CC1: 0085 Oatmeal Heather 1 (1, 1) ball or 20 (20, 40) m
CC2: 9958 Light Indigo 2 (2, 2) balls or 120 (140, 180) m
CC3: 0008 Light Denim 1 (1, 1) ball or 30 (40, 60) m
CC4: 1235 Ray of Light 1 (1, 1) ball or 20 (30, 40) m

Needles: Circular needles (40 and 80 cm/16 and 32 in) and double-pointed needles in size 6 mm (US 10).

You will also need: Stitch markers, waste yarn or stitch holders, and a tapestry needle.

Tension (gauge): 14 sts and 19 rows = 10 × 10 cm (4 × 4 in) in stocking (stockinette) stitch, lightly blocked.

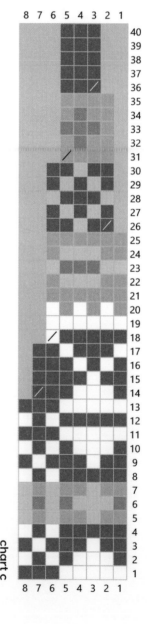

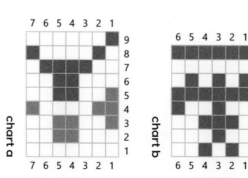

SLEEVES

Using 6 mm needles and MC, cast on 40 (40, 44) sts. Join in the round, ensuring not to twist the row of stitches. PM.

Ribbing: *K2, p2, repeat from * to end.

Repeat this round 14 more times. On the last round of ribbing, increase by 2 (9, 12) sts. You should now have 42 (49, 56) sts.

Follow chart A: Using MC and CCs 1 and 2, work the rows of the chart in stocking stitch. The pattern repeats 6 (7, 8) times. Once you have completed all 9 rounds of chart A, cut the CCs.

Increase round: Using MC, *k1 M1L, knit until 1 st before round marker, M1R, k1.

Work in stocking stitch for 7 (7, 6) rounds.**

Repeat from * to ** a further 5 (5, 7) times.

You should now have 54 (61, 72) sts.

Complete the sleeve: Using MC, continue working in the round in stocking stitch until sleeve measures 42 (44, 46) cm (16½ (17⅜, 18⅛) in) OR is 4 cm (1½ in) shorter than the desired length from cuff to armpit.

Follow chart B: Using MC and CC2, work the rows of chart B in stocking stitch. (Note that, **for size M only**, you need to decrease 1 st at the start of row 1 so you are working with a stitch count of 60 sts.) The pattern repeats 9 (10, 12) times per round.

Next round: Using CC2, knit to 5 (5, 6) sts before the marker. Transfer the remaining 5 (5, 6) sts to waste yarn, RM, then transfer the first 5 (5, 6) sts of the round to the same waste yarn, reserving a total of 10 (10, 12) sts for the armpit, leaving 44 (50, 60) sts on the needles for the sleeve.

Set aside and knit the remaining sleeve in the same way.

BODY

Using 6 mm needles and MC, cast on 124 (140, 160) sts. Join in the round, ensuring not to twist the row of stitches. PM.

Ribbing: *K2, p2, repeat from * to end.

Repeat this round 14 more times. On the last round of ribbing, increase 2 (0, 1) st(s) at even intervals. You will now have 126 (140, 161) sts. Add another stitch marker after 63 (70, 81) stitches as a side marker.

Follow chart A: Using MC and CC2, work the rows of the chart. The pattern repeats 18 (20, 23) times. When you have completed all 9 rounds of the chart, cut the CCs.

Decrease round: Using MC, knit to end, decreasing 0 (2, 5) sts at even intervals. (Note, **size L only**, decrease 1 st from before the side marker, and 2 sts after the side marker, so you end with an equal number of sts on either side of the side marker.) You should now have 126 (138, 156) sts.

Continue working in the round in stocking stitch until the body measures 42 (44, 46) cm (16½ (17⅜, 18⅛) in) OR is 4 cm (1½ in) shorter than the desired length from hem to armpit.

Follow chart B: Using MC and CC2, work the rows of chart B in stocking stitch. The pattern repeats 21 (23, 26) times.

YOKE

Join the body and sleeves: Using CC2, knit stitches from the body to 5 (5, 6) sts before the side marker. Transfer the next 10 (10, 12) sts to waste yarn (remove the side marker). PM (this is the new round marker). Transfer the 44 (50, 60) sts for one sleeve onto needles and knit them. Next, knit the body stitches to 5 (5, 6) sts before the marker. Transfer the next 10 (10, 12) sts to waste yarn (remove the original round marker). Now transfer the 44 (50, 60) sts for the remaining sleeve onto needles and knit them, then continue to the new round marker (this is now positioned at the join between the back section and left sleeve) You should now have 194 (218, 252) sts.

Decrease round: Using CC2, work 1 round in stocking stitch, decreasing 2 (2, 4) sts at even intervals. You should now have 192 (216, 248) sts. Note, if you would like a deeper yoke, you can continue in CC2 until the yoke has the desired depth before beginning chart C.

Follow chart C: Using MC and CCs 1, 2, 3, and 4, work the rows of chart C, making decreases as indicated. The chart repeats 24 (27, 31) times per round. When you have completed all 40 rows of the chart, you should have 72 (81, 93) sts.

NECK

Knit a small elevation in the back using short rows. Begin by marking the mid-back with a stitch marker. Then, Using CC2, knit to the marker and continue as follows:

Row 1 (RS): K12 (16, 18) sts, turn work.
Row 2 (WS): Slip 1 st, p23 (31, 35) sts, turn work.
Row 3: Slip 1 st, k33 (41, 45) sts, turn work.
Row 4: Slip 1 st, p43 (51, 55) sts, turn work.
Row 5: Knit to round marker.
Using CC2, continue working in stocking stitch for 2 more rounds. Cast (bind) off using a stretchy cast-off method.

FINISHING

Sew all the ends into the wrong side of the work. Graft the armpit stitches. Wet the sweater and then squeeze dry. Shape and lay flat to dry.

> " Many people worry about white wool becoming dirty easily. If it does, first let the sweater dry, then scratch away the worst of the dirt. This often works well because dirt does not attach easily to wool. Airing is a great way to clean your woollen garments. If that doesn't help, you can wash the sweater by hand in cold water, or use a wool or handwash programme on your washing machine.

"

The Sammalpolku sweater's forest hues and soft mossy patterns create a striking result that looks good on both men and women. The sweater is knitted from the hem up and is easier to manage than many stranded-knitting patterns due to the fact that there are few longer floats to deal with, preventing long loops of yarn on the inside of the sweater that could catch when you put it on.

Sammalpolku (Mossy Path)

DESIGNER PIRJO IIVONEN

SAMMALPOLKU (MOSSY PATH)

MODEL SHOWN IS SIZE M

Sizes: S (M, L, XL)
Recommended ease 4 cm (1½ in).

Dimensions of finished sweater:
Chest circumference: 85.5 (93.5, 101, 109) cm (33⅝ (36¾, 39¾, 42⅞) in).
Length from armpit to hem: 40 (42, 45, 48) cm (15¾ (16½, 17¾, 18⅞) in).
Length from front collar to hem: 61.5 (64.5, 68.5, 73) cm (24¼ (25⅜, 27, 28¾) in).
Circumference of upper sleeve: 35.5 (38, 40, 42) cm (14 (15, 15¾, 16½) in).
Wrist circumference: 22 (24.5, 26.5, 26.5) cm (8⅝ (9⅝, 10½, 10½) in).
Inner sleeve length: 45 (48, 51, 53) cm (17¾ (18⅞, 20⅛, 20⅞) in).

Yarn (see conversions on page 11): Wetterhoff Wanja (100% wool; 100 m/50 g) or equivalent Aran/Worsted weight yarn.
MC: 1142 Tummanharmaa 7 (8, 10, 12) balls or 700 (800, 1000, 1200) m
CC: 1187 Vaaleanvihreä 4 (5, 6, 7) balls or 400 (500, 600, 700) m

Needles: Circular needles (80 and 100 cm/32 and 40 in) and double-pointed needles in sizes 3.5 mm (US 4) and 4 mm (US 6).

You will also need: Stitch markers, waste yarn or stitch holders, and a tapestry needle.

Tension (gauge): 18 sts and 23 rows = 10 × 10 cm (4 x 4 in) in stocking (stockinette) stitch, lightly blocked.

chart a

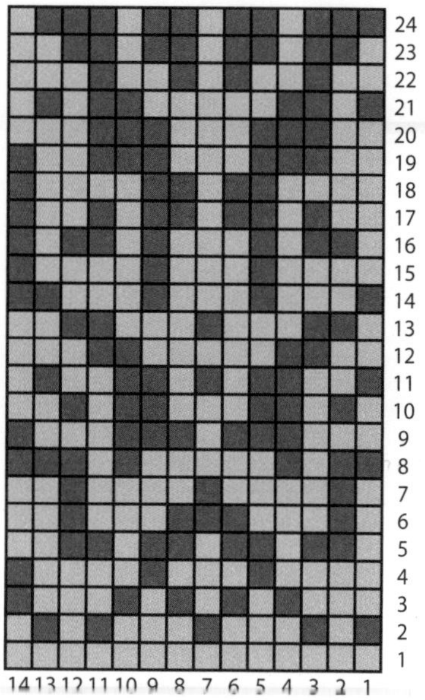

MC
CC
k2tog
ssk
repeat pattern
size S sleeves
size M sleeves
sizes L and XL sleeves
sleeve increases

chart b

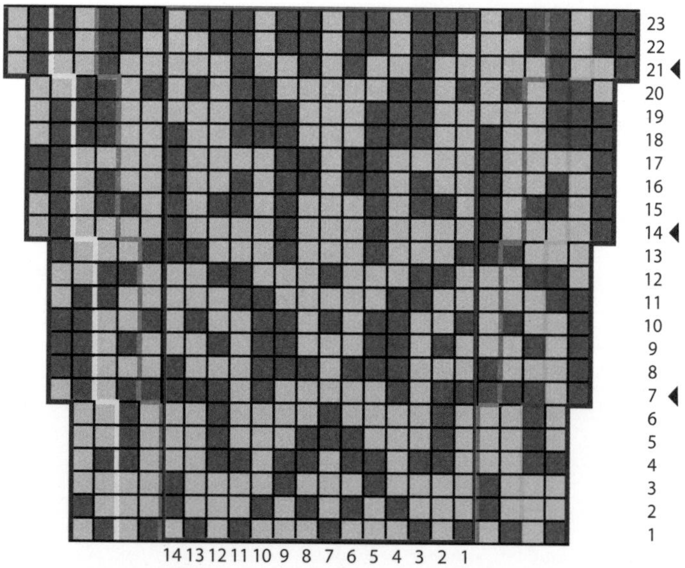

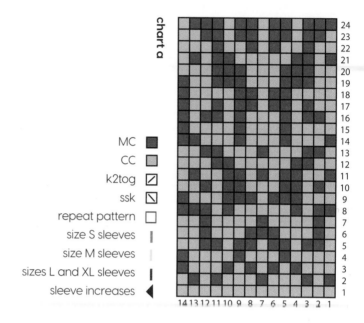

BODY

Using 3.5 mm needles and CC, cast on 154 (168, 182, 196) sts. Join in the round, being careful not to twist the row of stitches. PM (this is positioned at the mid back of the sweater.

Ribbing: *K1 tbl, p1, repeat from * to end.
Repeat this round until ribbing measures 5 cm (2 in).

Follow chart A: Switch to 4 mm needles. Using MC and CC, work the rows of the chart in stocking stitch. The pattern repeats 11 (12, 13, 14) times per round. Once you've knitted all 24 rows of the chart, cut CC.

Complete the body: Using MC, continue working in the round in stocking stitch until the body measures 40 (42,45,48) cm (15¾ (16½, 17¾, 18¾) in) from the cast-on edge. Set aside the body and knit the sleeves.

SLEEVES

Using 3.5 mm needles and CC, cast on 40 (44, 48, 48) sts. Join in the round, ensuring not to twist the row of stitches. PM (this is positioned at the inner sleeve).

Ribbing: *K1 tbl, p1, repeat from * to end.
Repeat this round until ribbing measures 5 cm (2 in). Switch to 4 mm needles.

Increase round: K1, M1R, knit to 1 st before marker, M1L, k1. You should now have 42 (46, 50, 50) sts.

Follow chart B: Using MC and CC, work the rows of the chart in stocking stitch. The basic pattern repeat is outlined in red. Please note that the edges of the chart are outlined:
in blue **for size S only**
in yellow **for size M only**
in purple **for sizes L and XL only.**

The pattern repeats 3 times per round. **For size S only,** the number of stitches for the first 7 rows allows for exactly 3 repeats. **For sizes M, L and XL,** there are a few stitches at the beginnings and ends of the rounds on either side of the 3 pattern repeats. To work the increases on rows 7, 14, and 21 of chart B, work as follows: knit the first st on the left needle in the colour shown on the chart for the first stitch on that row. Next, M1R using the colour shown on the chart for the second stitch on that row. Follow the chart until the first pattern repeat is completed, then work the remaining 2 pattern repeats on that row. To end the row, follow the chart beyond st 14 on the pattern repeat until 1 st remains. M1L in the colour marked on the chart for the penultimate stitch in that row, then knit the final stitch in the colour marked on the chart for the final stitch on that row. Once you have knitted all 24 rows of the chart, you should have 48 (52, 56, 56) sts, cut the MC. Using 4 mm needles and MC, knit 4 rounds.

Continue the sleeve increases:

Next round: M1L, knit to 1 st before marker, M1R, k1. *[2 sts increased – 50 (54, 58, 58 in total)]*
Repeat this increase round once every 3 (3, 2.5, 2.5) cm (1¼ (1¼, 1, 1) in) a further 8 (8, 8, 10) times. You should now have 64 (68, 72, 76) sts.

Complete the sleeve: Continue knitting in stocking stitch until the sleeve measures 45 (48, 51, 53) cm (17¾ (18⅞, 20⅛, 20⅞) in) from cast-on edge. Transfer the first 4 (5, 6, 7) and final 3 (4, 5, 6) sts of the round to waste yarn to reserve a total of 7 (9, 11, 13) sts for the armpit. You should now have 57 (59, 61, 63) sts on the needles for the sleeve.

Set aside and knit the other sleeve in the same way.

YOKE

Join the body and sleeves: Using 4 mm needles and MC, k 35 (37, 40, 42) sts from the body for the back left section, then transfer the next 7 (9, 11, 13) sts to waste yarn for the left armpit. Now join the first sleeve by knitting the 57 (59, 61, 63) sts. K70 (76, 80, 86) sts from the body for the front section, then transfer the next 7 (9, 11, 13) sts to waste yarn for the right armpit. Join the second sleeve by knitting the 57 (59, 61, 63) sts. Knit the final 35 (37, 40, 42) sts from the body for the back right section to complete the round. You should now have 254 (268, 282, 296) sts.

Decrease round 1: Knit until there is 1 st left on the left sleeve, k2tog, knit until there is 1 st left on the right sleeve, k2tog, knit to end of round. You should now have 252 (266, 280, 294) sts.

Complete the yoke: Using MC, continue working in the round in stocking stitch for another 0 (2, 4, 8) rounds. Note that you can adjust the depth of the yoke by either increasing or decreasing the number of rounds you knit before working chart C.

Follow chart C: Using MC and CC, work the rows of chart C, making decreases as indicated. The pattern repeats 18 (19, 20, 21) times per round. Once you have completed all 48 rows of the chart, cut the MC. You should now have 90 (95, 100, 105) sts and the depth of the yoke is 21.5 (22.5, 23.5, 25) cm (8½ (8⅞, 9¼, 9⅞) in).

NECK

Switch to 3.5 mm needles. Using CC, knit a small elevation in the back using short rows as follows:

Row 1 (RS): K10, turn work.

Row 2 (WS): Make a DS, purl to round marker, SM, p10, turn work.

Row 3: Make a DS, knit to round marker, SM, knit to DS, knit the DS as a single stitch, k5, turn work.

Row 4: Make a DS, purl to round marker, SM, purl to DS, purl the DS as a single stitch, p5, turn work.

Row 5: Make a DS, knit to round marker, SM, knit to DS, knit the DS as a single stitch, k5, turn work.

Row 6: Make a DS, purl to round marker, SM, purl to DS, purl the DS as a single stitch, p5, turn work.

Row 7: Make a DS, knit to round marker, SM, knit to DS, knit the DS as a single stitch, k5, turn work.

Row 8: Make a DS, purl to round marker, SM, purl to DS, purl the DS as a single stitch, p5, turn work.

Row 9: Make a DS, knit to round marker.

Next round: Knit 1 round, knitting each DS on the row as a single stitch.

Decrease round:

Size S only: K4, (k2tog, k7) 9 times, k2tog, k3. *[10 sts decreased – 80 sts remaining]*

Size M only: K3, (k2tog, k4) 5 times, (k2tog, k5) 4 times, (k2tog, k4) 5 times, k2tog, k2. *[15 sts decreased – 80 sts remaining]*

Size L only: K3, (k2tog, k4) 6 times, (k2tog, k5) 3 times, (k2tog, k4) 6 times, k2tog, k2. *[16 sts decreased – 84 sts remaining]*

Size XL only: K2, (k2tog, k3) 20 times, k2tog, k1. *[21 sts decreased – 84 sts remaining]*

Ribbing: *K1 tbl, p1, repeat from * to end.

Repeat this round until ribbing measures 2 cm (¾ in) OR the neck is the desired length.

Next round: Cast (bind) off using a stretchy cast-off method, such as the following:

K1, yo, p1, skpo (move both the yo and the knit stitch over the purl stitch simultaneously), *k1, skpo, yo, p1, skpo, repeat from * until you have cast off all stitches.

FINISHING

Graft the armpits and sew the ends into the wrong side of the work. Wash the sweater in lukewarm water, squeeze inside a towel to remove excess water, shape on a flat surface, and leave to dry.

chart c

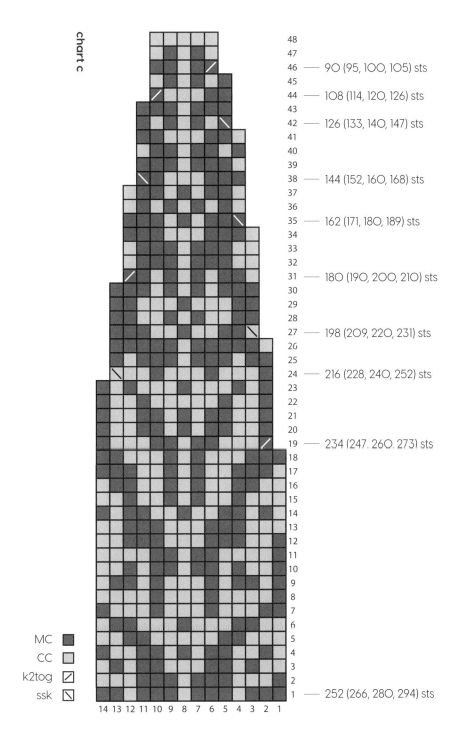

48
47
46 —— 90 (95, 100, 105) sts
45
44 —— 108 (114, 120, 126) sts
43
42 —— 126 (133, 140, 147) sts
41
40
39
38 —— 144 (152, 160, 168) sts
37
36
35 —— 162 (171, 180, 189) sts
34
33
32
31 —— 180 (190, 200, 210) sts
30
29
28
27 —— 198 (209, 220, 231) sts
26
25
24 —— 216 (228, 240, 252) sts
23
22
21
20
19 —— 234 (247, 260, 273) sts
18
17
16
15
14
13
12
11
10
9
8
7
6
5
4
3
2
1 —— 252 (266, 280, 294) sts

14 13 12 11 10 9 8 7 6 5 4 3 2 1

MC ■
CC ☐
k2tog ◰
ssk ◳

"

The scent of mossy tussocks, the flavour of autumn berries, and the magic of the forest shade are all knitted into this sweater. If you look closely, you might spot the family of foxes peeping out from their hiding places in the undergrowth. This sweater is knitted in the round from neck to hem.

Siimes (Shade)

DESIGNER NIINA LAITINEN

SIIMES (SHADE)

MODEL SHOWN IS SIZE M

Sizes: S (M, L, XL)
Recommended positive ease 4 cm (1½ in).

Dimensions of finished sweater:
Chest circumference: 95.5 (104.5, 112, 120) cm (37⅝ (41⅛, 44⅛, 47¼) in).
Length from armpit to hem: 39 (39, 40, 41) cm (15⅜ (15⅜, 15¾, 16⅛) in).
Length from front collar to hem: 63 (63.5, 64.5, 66) cm (24¾ (25, 25⅜, 26) in).
Circumference of upper sleeve: 34.5 (35.5, 38, 40) cm (13⅝ (14, 15, 15¾) in).
Wrist circumference: 23.5 (23.5, 24.5, 25.5) cm (9¼, 9¼, 9⅝, 10) in).
Inner sleeve length: 48 (49, 50, 50) cm (18⅞ (19¼, 19⅝, 19⅝) in).

Yarn (see conversions on page 11): Novita Icelandic Wool (100% wool; 90 m/50 g) or equivalent Aran/Worsted weight yarn.
MC: 010 Luonnonvalkoinen 8 (9, 10, 11) balls or 720 (810, 900, 990) m
CC1: 384 Mänty 3 (3, 4, 4) balls or 270 (270, 360, 360) m
CC2: 638 Seitikki 2 (2, 3, 3) balls or 180 (180, 270, 270) m

Needles: Circular needles (40 and 80 cm/16 and 32 in) and double-pointed needles in sizes in sizes 4 mm (US 6) and 4.5 mm (US 7).

You will also need: Stitch markers, waste yarn or stitch holders, and a tapestry needle.

Tension (gauge): 18 sts and 24 rows = 10 × 10 cm (4 x 4 in) in stocking (stockinette) stitch, lightly blocked.

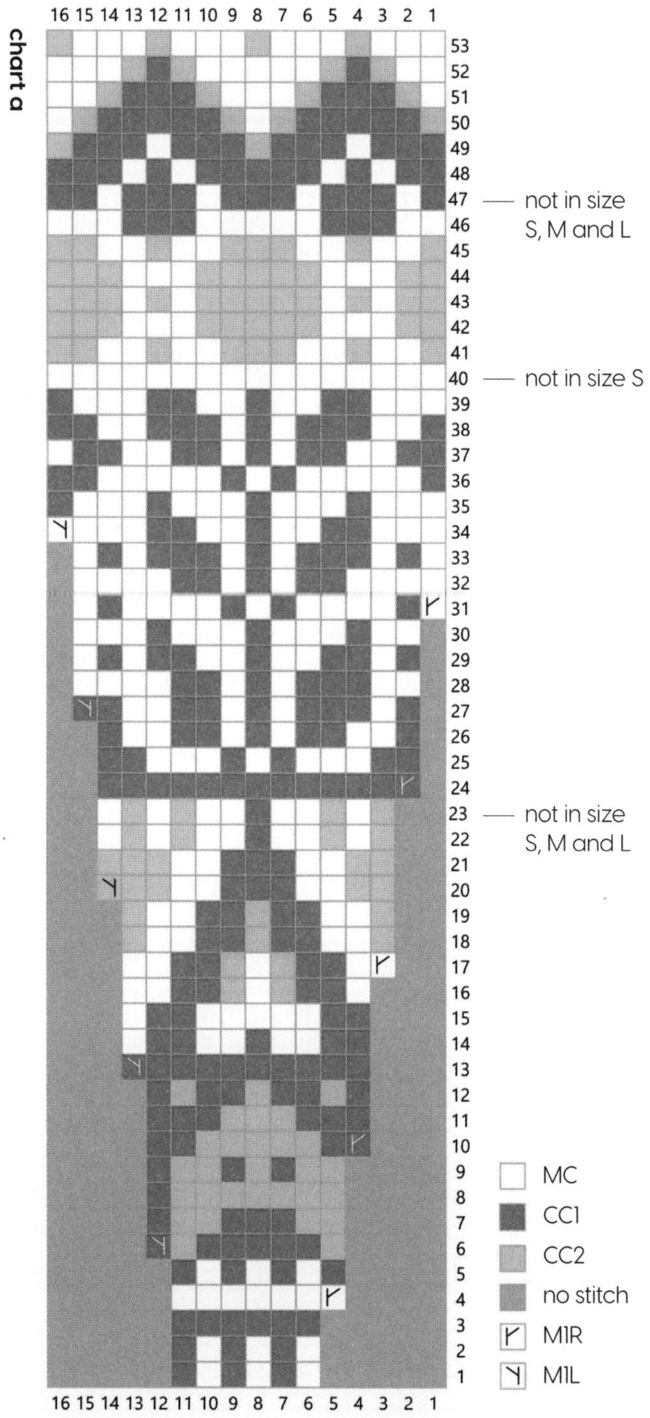
chart a
16 15 14 13 12 11 10 9 8 7 6 5 4 3 2 1
53 52 51 50 49 48 47 46 45 44 43 42 41 40 39 38 37 36 35 34 33 32 31 30 29 28 27 26 25 24 23 22 21 20 19 18 17 16 15 14 13 12 11 10 9 8 7 6 5 4 3 2 1
47 — not in size S, M and L
40 — not in size S
23 — not in size S, M and L
MC
CC1
CC2
no stitch
MIR
MIL

YOKE

Using 4 mm circular needles and MC, cast on 82 (84, 86, 88) sts. Join in the round, being careful not to twist the row of stitches. PM.

Ribbing: *K1 tbl, p1, repeat from * to end. Repeat this round until ribbing measures 3 cm (1¼ in). Swap to the thicker needles and knit 3 rounds of stockinette in the MC. On the first round, increase 14 (18, 22, 26) sts at even intervals = 96 (102, 108, 114) sts.

Follow chart A: Using MC, CC1 and CC2, work the rows of the chart beginning at row 2 for sizes S and M.

Repeat the 16-stitch pattern 16 (17, 18, 19) times per round. Work all rows of the chart for your size and make increases at the points indicated on the chart.

For size S only: Skip chart rows 23, 40 and 47.

For sizes M and L only: Skip chart rows 23 and 47. Once you have completed all chart rows for your size, you should have 256, (272, 288, 304) sts. Cut CCs 1 and 2.

Next round: Using MC and 4.5 mm needles, knit 1 round.

Next round: Increase 0, (0, 2, 4) sts at even intervals. You should now have 256 (272, 290, 308) sts. If necessary, continue working in stocking stitch until the depth of the yoke when measured after the ribbing is 21 (21.5, 21.5, 22) cm (8¼ (8½, 8½, 8⅝) in).

Separate the sleeves: K76 (83, 89, 95) sts for the back, transfer the next 52 (53, 56, 59) sts to waste yarn to reserve for the left sleeve, cast on 10 (11, 12, 13) sts for the left armpit, k76 (83, 89, 95) sts, transfer the next 52 (53, 56, 59) sts to waste yarn to reserve for the right sleeve, cast on 10 (11, 12, 13) sts for the right armpit. You should now have 172 (188, 202, 216) sts, and the marker is positioned where the right sleeve and right back meet.

BODY

Using 4.5 mm needles and MC, continue working in stocking stitch until the body measures 33 (33, 34, 35) cm (13 (13, 13⅜, 13¾) in) from the armpit.

Next round: Switch to 4 mm needles. *K1 tbl, p1, repeat from * to end. Repeat this round until ribbing measures 6 cm (2⅜ in). Cast (bind) off in rib using a stretchy cast-off method.

SLEEVES

Transfer the 52 (53, 56, 59) sts you reserved for one sleeves onto 4.5 mm needles. Using MC, pick up and knit 10 (11, 12, 13) sts from the armpit. PM at the midway point of the newly picked-up stitches. You should now have 62 (64, 68, 72) sts. Work in the round in stocking stitch for 2 cm (¾ in).

Decrease round: K2, k2tog, knit to last 4 sts, ssk or skpo, k2. Repeat this decrease round once every 3.5 (3.5, 3, 2.5) cm (1⅜ (1⅜, 1¼, 1) in) a further 9 (10, 11, 12) times. You should now have 42 (42, 44, 46) sts. Continue working in the round in stocking stitch until the sleeve measures 42 (43, 44, 44) cm from the armpit.

Ribbing: Switch to 4 mm needles. *K1 tbl, p1, repeat from * to end. Repeat this round until ribbing measures 6 cm (2⅜ in). Cast (bind) off in rib using a stretchy cast-off method. Knit the other sleeve in the same way.

FINISHING

Sew in the ends. Place the sweater on a flat surface inside out, steam lightly, and let dry.

As the name suggests, you'll find heaps of lovely hearts all around this sweater's stranded-knitted yoke. The pretty patterns invite you to knit a strip of pink flowers among them. Sydänmaa is a quick knit, the patterns are easy, and the sweater almost knits itself after the yoke. It is knitted in the round from neck to hem.

Sydänmaa (Heartland)

DESIGNER NIINA LAITINEN

SYDÄNMAA (HEARTLAND)

MODEL SHOWN IS SIZE M

Sizes: S (M, L, XL)

Recommended positive ease 4 cm (1½ in).

Dimensions of finished sweater:

Chest circumference: 95.5 (104.5, 112, 120) cm 37⅝ (41⅛, 44⅛, 47¼) in).

Length from armpit to hem: 39 (39, 40, 41) cm (15⅜ (15⅜, 15¾, 16⅛) in).

Length from front collar to hem: 63 (63.5, 64.5, 66) cm (24¾ (25, 25⅜, 26) in).

Circumference of upper sleeve: 34.5 (35.5, 38, 40) cm (13⅝ (14, 15, 15¾) in).

Wrist circumference: 22 (22, 24.5, 26.5) cm (8⅝ (8⅝, 9⅝, 10½) in).

Inner sleeve length: 48 (49, 50, 50) cm (18⅞ (19¼, 19⅝, 19⅝) in).

Yarn (see conversions on page 11): Novita Icelandic Wool (100% wool; 90 m/50 g) or equivalent Aran/Worsted weight yarn.

MC: 044 Grafiitti 8 (9, 10, 11) balls or 720 (810, 900, 990) m

CC1: 010 Luonnonvalkoinen 3 (3, 4, 4) balls or 270 (270, 360, 360) m

CC2: 550 Pioni 2 (2, 3, 3) balls or 180 (180, 270, 270) m

Needles: Circular needles (40 and 80 cm/16 and 32 in) and double-pointed needles in sizes 4 mm (US 6) and 4.5 mm (US 7).

You will also need: Stitch markers, waste yarn or stitch holders, and a tapestry needle.

Tension (gauge): 18 sts and 24 rows = 10 × 10 cm (4 x 4 in) in stocking (stockinette) stitch, lightly blocked.

chart a

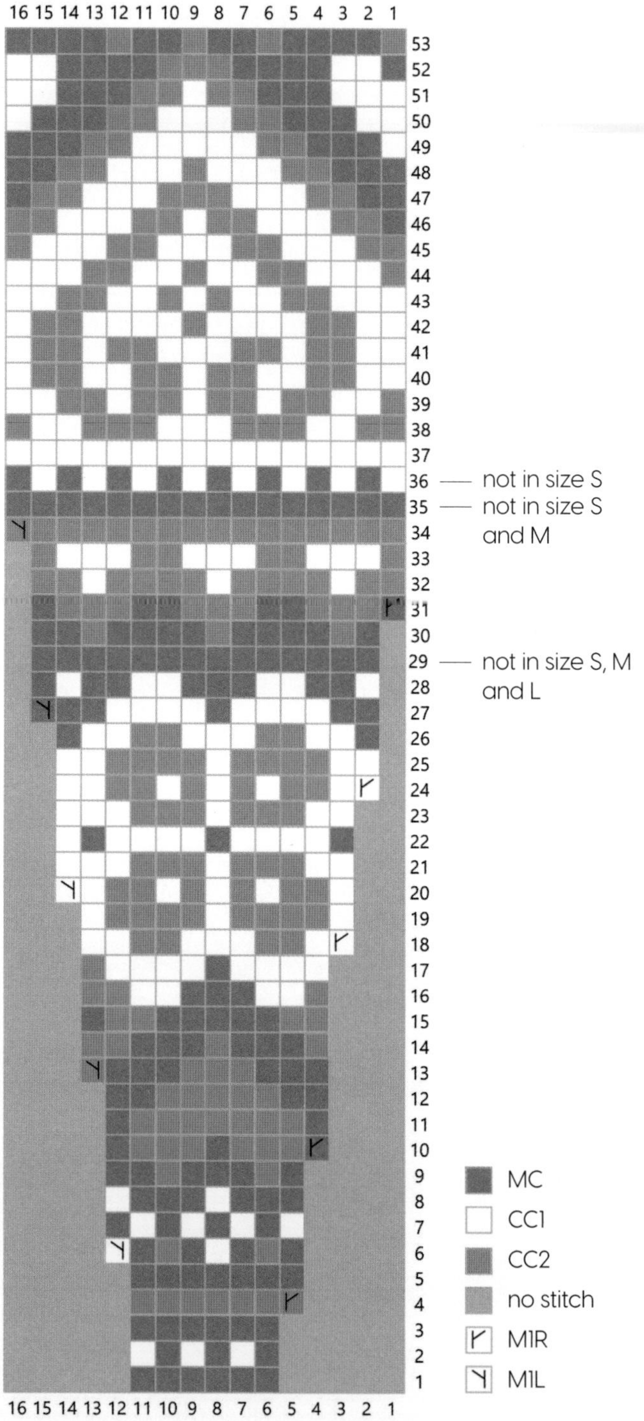

not in size S
not in size S and M
not in size S, M and L
MC
CC1
CC2
no stitch
M1R
M1L

YOKE

Using 4 mm needles and MC, cast on 80 (84, 88, 88) sts. Join the work in the round, being careful not to twist the row of stitches. PM.

Ribbing: *K2, p2, repeat from * to end.

Repeat this round until ribbing measures 3 cm (1¼ in).

Increase round: Switch to 4.5 mm needles. Using MC, work in stocking stitch for 1 round, increasing 16 (18, 20, 26) sts at even intervals. You should now have 96 (102, 108, 114) sts.

Work 2 more rounds in stocking stitch.

Follow chart A: Using MC and CCs 1 and 2, work the rows of chart A in stocking stitch, making increases as indicated. The pattern begins with 6 sts and repeats 16 (17, 18, 19) times per round. Please note: for size S only, skip chart rows 29, 35, and 36; for size M only, skip chart rows 29 and 35; for size L only, skip chart row 29. After completing the chart you should have 256, (272, 288, 304) sts. Cut the CCs. Using MC, knit 1 round in stocking stitch.

Increase round: Work in stocking stitch to the end of the round, increasing 0 (0, 2, 4) sts at even intervals. You should now have 256 (272, 290, 308) sts.

If necessary, continue working in the round in stocking stitch until the depth of the yoke when measured after the ribbing is 21 (21.5, 21.5, 22) cm (8¼ (8½, 8½, 8⅝) in.

Separate the sleeves: K76 (83, 89, 95) sts for the back section, transfer the next 52 (53, 56, 59) sts to waste yarn for the left sleeve, cast on 10 (11, 12, 13) sts for the left armpit, k76 (83, 89, 95) sts for the front section, transfer the next 52 (53, 56, 59) sts to waste yarn for the right sleeve, then cast on 10 (11, 12, 13) sts for the right armpit. You should now have 172 (188, 202, 216) sts.

BODY

Using 4.5 mm needles and MC, continue working in the round in stocking stitch until the body measures 33 (33, 34, 35) cm (13 (13, 13½, 14) in).

Decrease round (size L only): Work 1 round in stocking stitch, decreasing 2 sts at even intervals. *[2 sts decreased – 200 sts remaining]*

Ribbing: Switch to 4 mm needles. *K2, p2, repeat from * to end.

Repeat this round until ribbing measures 6 cm (2⅜ in). Cast (bind) off using a stretchy cast-off method.

SLEEVES

Transfer the 52 (53, 56, 59) sts you reserved for one of the sleeves onto 4.5 mm needles. Using MC, pick up and knit 10 (11, 12, 13) sts from the armpit. PM at the midway point of the newly picked-up stitches. You should now have 62 (64, 68, 72) sts.

Work in the round in stocking stitch for 2 cm (¾ in).

Decrease round: K2, k2tog, knit to last 4 sts, ssk or skpo, k2.

Repeat this decrease row once every 3 cm (1¼ in) a further 10 (11, 11, 11) times. You should now have 40 (40, 44, 48) sts.

Continue working in the round in stocking stitch until the sleeve measures 42 (43, 44, 44) cm (16½ (17, 17⅜, 17⅜) in) from the armpit.

Ribbing: Switch to 4 mm needles. *K2, p2, repeat from * to end.

Repeat this round until ribbing measures 6 cm (2⅜ in). Cast (bind) off in rib using a stretchy cast-off method. Knit the other sleeve in the same way.

FINISHING

Sew in the ends on the wrong side. Place the sweater on a flat surface inside out, steam lightly, and let dry.

DESIGNERS

PIRJO IIVONEN

Unelmien silmukat – haaveista sukiksi (2015)
   (Dream stitches – from dream to sock)
Unelmien huivit (2017) (Dream scarves)
Suuri suomalainen toivesukkakirja –
   miesten sukat (2018)
   (The big Finnish book of socks – men's socks)
Unelmien neuleasusteet (2018)
   (Dream knitted accessories)
Jämälankasukat –
   Neulo keränloput ihaniksi sukiksi! (2019)
   (Socks from waste yarn – Knit your scrap yarn
   into beautiful socks!)
Suuri suomalainen toivesukkakirja –
   lasten sukat (2019)
   (The big Finnish book of socks – children's socks)
Suuri suomalainen toivesukkakirja –
   pitkät sukat (2020)
   (The big Finnish book of socks – long socks)
Unelmien talvineuleet (2021) (Dream winter knits)
Suuri suomalainen toivesukkakirja –
   sukat kaikilla mausteilla (2021)
   (The big Finnish book of socks – socks with
   everything)

FB Unelmien silmukat
IG unelmiensilmukat
RAVELRY Siniusvan

TIINA KAARELA

Puikkomaisterin sukkakirja (2015)
   (The needlemaster's sock book)
Puikkomaisterin lapaskirja (2016)
   (The needlemaster's mitten book)
Puikkomaisterin pipokirja (2017)
   (The needlemaster's woolly hat book)
Puikkomaisterin sukkasirkus (2018)
   (The needlemaster's sock circus)
Suuri suomalainen toivesukkakirja –
   miesten sukat (2018)
   (The big Finnish book of socks – men's socks)
Suuri suomalainen toivesukkakirja –
   lasten sukat (2019)
   (The big Finnish book of socks – children's socks)
Suuri suomalainen toivesukkakirja –
   pitkät sukat (2020)
   (The big Finnish book of socks – long socks)
Suuri suomalainen toivesukkakirja –
   sukat kaikilla mausteilla (2021)
   (The big Finnish book of socks – socks
   with everything)

FB Puikkomaisteri
IG puikkomaisteri

ANNIKA KONTTANIEMI

IG annika_konttaniemi
RAVELRY Akonttaniemi
YOUTUBE Annika Konttaniemi

NIINA LAITINEN

Villasukkien vuosi (2018) (Knitted socks from Finland
   – 20 Nordic designs for all year round)
Suuri suomalainen toivesukkakirja –
   miesten sukat (2018)
   (The big Finnish book of socks – men's socks)
Kaikkien aikojen villasukat –
   90-vuotiaan Novitan juhlakirja (2018)
   (Timeless woollen socks – celebrating Novita's
   90th anniversary)
Satumaiset silmukat (2019) (Fairytale stitches)
Suuri suomalainen toivesukkakirja –
   lasten sukat (2019)
   (The big Finnish book of socks – children's socks)
Villasukkien uusi vuosi (2020)
   (A new year for woollen socks)
Suuri suomalainen toivesukkakirja –
   pitkät sukat (2020)
   (The big Finnish book of socks – long socks)
Lempivillasukkia (2021) (Popular woollen socks)

Suuri suomalainen toivesukkakirja –
   sukat kaikilla mausteilla (2021)
   (The big Finnish book of socks – socks
   with everything)

www.niinalaitinendesigns.com
FB Niina Laitinen designs
FB GROUP Taimitarha
IG niinalaitinendesigns

MERJA OJANPERÄ

Kauneimmat villasukat (2016)
   (The most beautiful woollen socks)
Näyttävimmät villasukat (2017)
   (The most eye-catching woollen socks)
Sydämellinen sukkakirja (2018)
   (A heartfelt sock book)
Suuri suomalainen toivesukkakirja –
   miesten sukat (2018)
   (The big Finnish book of socks – men's socks)
Kauneimmat neuleet (2019) (The most beautiful knits)
Suuri suomalainen toivesukkakirja –
   lasten sukat (2019)
   (The big Finnish book of socks – children's socks)
Neuleita vauvalle (2019) (Knitwear for babies)
Rakkaudesta villasukkiin (2020)
   (A love for woollen socks)
Pitsisukkien taikaa (2021) (The magic of lace socks)

www.merjadesign.com
FB hyvatsilmukat
IG merjaojanpera

SOILE PYHÄNNISKA

IG s.pyhanniska

ANNA-KAROLIINA TETRI

Luonnonvärjäys (2008) (Natural dyeing)
Huovutus (2011) (Felting)
Sienivärjäys (2013) (Dyeing with mushrooms)
Huovutetut lapaset (2013) (Felted mittens)
Perinteiset lapaset (2014) (Traditional mittens)
Perinteiset villasukat (2015)
   (Traditional woollen socks)
Tekstiilivärjäys (2016) (Textile dyeing)
Suuri suomalainen toivesukkakirja –
   miesten sukat (2018)
   (The big Finnish book of socks – men's socks)
Perinteiset neule – ja virkkuutyöt (2018)
   (Traditional knitting and crocheting)
Suuri suomalainen toivesukkakirja –
   lasten sukat (2019)
   (The big Finnish book of socks – children's socks)
Perinteiset villasukat 2 –
   Suurmiesten, -naisten ja kansalaisten sukkia (2019)
   (Traditional woollen socks 2 – Socks for great
   men, women and people)
Suuri suomalainen toivesukkakirja –
   pitkät sukat (2020)
   (The big Finnish book of socks – long socks)
Värjää ja neulo (2021) (Dye and knit)
Suuri suomalainen toivesukkakirja –
   sukat kaikilla mausteilla (2021)
   (The big Finnish book of socks – socks
   with everything)

www.tetridesign.com
FB Tetri Design
IG annakaroliinatetri

MINTTU WIKBERG

Suuri suomalainen toivesukkakirja –
   sukat kaikilla mausteilla (2021)
   (The big Finnish book of socks – socks
   with everything)

www.pawlymade.com
IG pawlymade
RAVELRY pawlymade